KNOWING
and GROWING
in
ASSURANCE
of FAITH

KNOWING
and GROWING
in
ASSURANCE
of FAITH

Joel R. Beeke

CHRISTIAN
FOCUS

Copyright © Joel R. Beeke 2017

paperback ISBN 978-1-7819-1300-0
epub ISBN 978-1-5271-0083-1
mobi ISBN 978-1-5271-0084-8

10 9 8 7 6 5 4 3 2 1

Published in 2017
by
Christian Focus Publications Ltd,
Geanies House, Fearn, Ross-shire,
IV20 1TW, Great Britain.

www.christianfocus.com

Cover design by
Daniel van Straaten

Printed and bound by
Bell and Bain, Glasgow

MIX
Paper from
responsible sources
FSC® C007785

Contents

Foreword. 7

Preface. 11

1. Why Is Assurance of Faith Important?. 15

2. Why Do Many Christians Lack Assurance?. 25

3. Is Assurance of Faith Biblical
   and Normative?. 43

4. Three Possibilities Concerning Assurance 55

5. Assurance from God's Promises 75

6. Assurance from Evidences of Grace 89

7. Assurance from the Holy Spirit's
   Witnessing Testimony 107

8. How to Cultivate Assurance. 121

9. Assurance Lost and Renewed. 143

10. The Spirit's Role in Assurance 157

11. Final Questions About Assurance. 177

12. Conclusion. 193

    Appendix 1 201

    Appendix 2 203

With heartfelt appreciation to
Paul Washer
a faithful friend, fearless preacher,
winner of souls, writer about assurance,
and daring hunter – both spiritually and naturally

FOREWORD

Am I a real Christian? There is not a true Christian who has not asked himself or herself that question, in fact every Christian should be examining his life to see if redemption is his or her privilege and eternal blessedness. As we come to the Lord's Supper, we do so renewing our awareness of our true condition and our thanks for the true condition of the blameless Son of God who became the Lamb of God and took away the sin of all who are joined to Him, even if that faith that joins them to Christ is as thin as a spider's thread. Oh that such a union of me a sinner, and Him the Savior, were mine for ever and ever!

Am I one such Christian? There is a Book that can help me. It is the Bible, the word that God has given us. It helps us first of all by telling us what a real Christian believes, that God is our Creator, that He is three persons, the Father, the Son, and the Holy Spirit, that this holy Father loved sinners in this groaning world so much that He sent His only begotten Son, Jehovah Jesus, to save us from the judgment that we deserve by His living on our behalf the life we have not been living, dying the death our sins deserve, exchanging our stony hearts for new hearts that love Him and want to serve Him perfectly. To those of us who put their trust in Him, God gives His Holy Spirit who strengthens and energizes us to live brand new lives that please and honor Him. We are enabled to fulfil our real end in living, to thus glorify God and enjoy Him. So, through our union with Christ we will be made fit to be declared righteous in the coming Judgment and be welcomed into the presence of the One before whom the angels hide their eyes and cry, 'Holy, holy, holy!'

This is what the Bible teaches a true Christian believes. Can you say, 'Well, I believe that, not perfectly alas, but these are the truths that are very, very important to me. This is what I want to hear from the pulpit whenever I attend church.' Then be encouraged! You believe what real Christians believe. You can enjoy no assurance of your salvation unless you believe these doctrines that God has taken such pains to give us in the Bible.

The Bible also tells me how a real Christian lives. He or she is in earnest about keeping the law of God. That law is first simply summarized in the Ten Commandments, but then it is amplified in Jesus' teaching in the Sermon on the Mount in Matthew 5–7. A Christian's behavior is also described in Romans 12 and Ephesians 5–6. Reading these parts of God's book sustains in every Christian two feelings: a longing to live that way and a sorrowful confession that his life does not match up and that he is so glad that the Lord Jesus' life did. He kept God's law. He was poor in spirit, and hungered and thirsted after righteousness; He was pure in heart, meek and lowly, and a peace maker. He lived like that in spite of the suffering it brought into His life. He loved His neighbor as Himself. He loved His enemies and prayed for them when they had nailed Him by His hands and feet to the cross. He did not overcome evil by evil; He overcame evil with good. That is the life every Christian esteems and admires: 'I want to live that life by the power of grace, but oh, how far short of attaining it I am!' Every Christian feels like that. No other way of life is attractive to him. His conscience convicts him when he falls short of the law of God in his inward desires, let alone in his outward behavior.

The book that God has given us defines for us what we are to believe and describes for us how we are to live. There can be no assurance that we are real Christians unless we will find some confidence in our hearts, some conviction, that these truths are what we want to believe and also this new heavenly conduct is how we want to live. These are the two foundations of attaining a feeling of assurance that we are the children of God. There can be no certainty without the desire to believe and behave as God has described for us.

But there is something more. God's Holy Spirit must inwardly deal with our minds as we consider these things, and our affections as we respond to the wonder of being sure that we have been saved by the grace of God, so that there can be occasional feelings of joy inexpressible that are created by the Spirit of God assuring us even on our worst days that we are real Christians behaving as we do. This is God's prerogative, His gift; it is God speaking to our inmost being, challenging our conduct, or He is telling us that He loves us and He wants us to feel loved.

It cannot be otherwise. We Christians make this claim that Father, Son, and Holy Spirit have come to us personally and individually and that the living God indwells us, that we have illimitable access to Him. Do you think we can have this absolute reality in the dispositional complex of our inmost beings – our hearts and souls – and not know of the indwelling God? Do you think it good or even possible to have Him for years in our lives and possess no conviction that He is there? A Christian is married to Christ. Would such a Christian not know the stirrings of affection of Christ as husband for the one the Savior loved and died for, to whose life the believer is joined for ever, whose body is His home, His temple?

How does the Lord of glory make Himself known to us? Certainly He does so by making us understand and believe and love the truths of Christian teaching. By Him we know what is true and what is erroneous. Certainly also God increases our assurance by making us hunger and thirst for righteousness, and sorrow over our daily sins. But there are also occasions when a certainty springs up in our hearts. We are reading the Bible and some words of promise are made peculiarly comforting and personal to us. Sometimes a light surprises the Christian while he sings. When we are hearing the preaching of the word we might be blessed with a renewal of joy at hearing of the Lord Jesus in the glory of His person and work as He is being offered to us in the gospel, and once again we receive Him by faith. Sometimes as we drive the car we may be overwhelmed with the love of God and need to stop. We can watch a sunset over the ocean, or look at the majesty of the Grand Canyon, or see our daughters talking seriously together listening intently and showing such affection to one another and the Spirit takes our love for them and they for us and overwhelms us with what His grace has given us. He gave us His Son and with His Son He freely has given to us – to me – every wonderful thing that has enriched my life.

I do not personally think of such moving experiences as being higher forms of assurance than those that come from reading the Bible and knowing that these truths are what I believe, or gaining from Scripture the confidence that this holy way of life is all my desire. They are just other wonderful privileges of the Christian life, a growing delightful relationship with a heavenly Father, and the best Friend, and the love of the Spirit for us.

These things are opened up for us more clearly and enjoyably by this most helpful book. This may well be the best of the many books that Dr Joel Beeke has written. It is an excellent introduction to Christian teaching on assurance. In this book a lamb may paddle and a hippopotamus may swim. The whole exercise of reading this book cannot create the very uncertainty that the author has sought so well to overcome. I am persuaded that there is no danger that in launching into this book you will close it with more doubts than when you began. None whatsoever. The book is an invitation. It is saying, 'Come now and read me, if you are trapped in a background of easy believism or trapped in the opposite fear of assurance being the certain mark of being presumptuous and so crushing the young shoots of hope and assurance as they appear.' Take and read me! Take and read now. You will come to no harm. Pray that you will be given deliverance from your doubts and have confidence to believe as the Biblical writers believed the honest and kindly promises that our one loving God has made to sinners whose hopes are in the lovely uniting one, who says, 'Come to me.'

GEOFF THOMAS

PREFACE

What is assurance of faith? Assurance of faith is the conviction that one belongs to Christ through faith and will enjoy everlasting salvation. A person who has assurance not only believes in Christ's righteousness as his salvation but knows that he believes and that he is graciously chosen, loved, and forgiven by God the Father for the sake of Christ Jesus, who has died for him and continues to pray for him in heaven. Such a person knows the Holy Spirit has regenerated him and continues to sanctify him. In other words, he believes not only the facts of the gospel that Jesus Christ saves sinners by His Spirit merely of grace, but he also believes that these facts apply to him personally – that he has a personal interest in the gospel and that all the blessings proclaimed in that gospel are his.

Such assurance is broad in terminology and scope. It is called 'full assurance of understanding'; 'full assurance of hope'; 'full assurance of faith' (Col. 2:2; Heb. 6:11, 18, 19; 10:22). It includes freedom from the guilt of sin, joy in relationship with the triune God, and a sense of belonging to the family of God. James W. Alexander said assurance 'carries with it the idea of fullness, such as of a tree laden with fruit, or of a vessel's sails when stretched by a favouring gale'.[1]

Personal assurance of faith is known by fruits such as close fellowship with God, childlike trust, willing obedience, thirsting after God, unspeakable joy and peace in the triune God for Christ's sake, and longing to glorify Him by carrying out the Great Commission.

---

1) J. W. Alexander, *Consolation in Discourses on Select Topics, Addressed to the Suffering People of God* (reprint, Ligonier, Pa.: Soli Deo Gloria, 1992), 138.

Assurance joyfully and prayerfully anticipates the renewal of all things in subjection to an eternal hope; assured believers view heaven as their home and long for the second advent of Christ and their translation to glory (2 Tim. 4:6-8).

I trust that the thrilling joys and abundant fruits of personal assurance of faith immediately show you how important this subject is. You can be a Christian without having assurance of faith, but your witness to Christ will be meager at best. To live the Christian life in a robust and blessed way, you need to have assurance of faith.

I was privileged to study the subject of assurance of faith intensely for several years while pursuing my PhD degree from Westminster Seminary in Philadelphia. I eventually published my doctoral dissertation as *Assurance of Faith: Calvin, English Puritanism, and the Dutch Second Reformation* (American University Studies, Series VII, Theology and Religion, vol. 89; New York: Peter Lang, 1991). Later, I simplified this work somewhat in my book *The Quest for Full Assurance: The Legacy of Calvin and His Successors* (Edinburgh: Banner of Truth Trust, 1999), and wrote several chapters and articles on the subject in various books and journals. Since then I have had numerous requests to write a simpler book on assurance for laypeople. So, when Christian Focus approached me to do just that, I immediately agreed to do so. In this book, though I have drawn from my other writings on this subject without bothering to footnote them often here, I have aimed to deal with this vast subject on a simpler and more practical level.

My prayer is that this book will impact people in a variety of ways: I pray that the strongly assured Christian will have his or her faith strengthened and increased, and will assist other Christians by speaking to them about the importance of obtaining assurance of faith and perhaps giving them a copy of this book! I pray that the weak Christian will cultivate assurance as a result of reading this book and will experience that his assurance is greatly enlarged by the Spirit's grace. I pray that the nominal Christians and unbelievers will realize what they are missing and will flee to Christ alone for salvation, and learn to find all their righteousness only in Him.

I wish to thank Misty Bourne, Ray Lanning, and John van Eyk for their editorial assistance, and of course, my wonderful queen, Mary, who spoils me by giving me all the love, friendship, encouragement, space, and time that I need to be a compulsive writer for my own soul – since I often feel closest to God when I write – and for the souls of others as well, including yours.

JOEL R. BEEKE

❧ 1 ❧

Why Is Assurance of
Faith Important?

'Assurance is the conscious confidence that we are in a right relation-ship with God through Christ', writes Sinclair Ferguson. 'It is the confidence that we have been justified and accepted by God in Christ, regenerated by his Spirit, and adopted into his family, and that through faith in him we will be kept for the day when our justification and adoption are consummated in the regeneration of all things.'[1]

Assurance has always been a vital subject for Christians. Its importance is more critical now because we live in a day of minimal assurance. Worse yet, many don't realize that. The desire to have fellowship with God, yearning for God's glory and heaven, and intercession for revival appear to be waning. That happens when the church's emphasis on earthly happiness overshadows her conviction that we are traveling through this world on our way to God and glory.

The need for a biblically-based doctrine of assurance is compounded by our culture's emphasis on feeling. How we feel often takes precedence over what we know or believe. This attitude has infiltrated the church. The dramatic growth of the charismatic

---

1) Sinclair B. Ferguson, 'The Reformation and Assurance', *The Banner of Truth*, cf. p. 30 fn. 1, no. 643 (Apr. 2017): 20.

movement can be attributed in part to a formal, lifeless Christianity, for the movement offers adherents emotional fulfillment and excitement to fill the void created by a lack of genuine assurance of faith and its fruits. Today we desperately need rich doctrinal thinking coupled with vibrant, sanctified living.

This book addresses the questions, difficulties, and issues associated with assurance of faith. Let's look first at eight important reasons for seeking to attain to and grow in assurance.

Soundness of Faith and Life

Our understanding of assurance of faith determines the soundness of our understanding of spiritual life. We can be orthodox in many areas and be unsound in our understanding of this key doctrine of Scripture.

Many people mistakenly assure themselves that they are Christians. They base their salvation on some form of presumption or 'easy believism'. In some cases, they claim that they have been saved from infancy but their lives do not bear the fruit of the Holy Spirit's sanctifying work. They may attend church faithfully, enjoy hearing gospel promises preached, participate in the sacraments, get involved in a few church ministries, do some outward good deeds for their neighbors, and live a decent and moral life, but, tested by the Beatitudes (Matt. 5:3-12), they are not spiritually poor in themselves; they do not mourn over sin, nor are they meek and submissive before God; they do not hunger and thirst after righteousness, etc. They rely on mere head knowledge of the gospel, and have not been born again (cf. John 3:5-8). They have never learned personally in their soul's experience before God that they are 'wretched, and miserable, and poor, and blind, and naked' (Rev. 3:17).

In many other cases, people claim they were born again based on an emotional response to a hyped-up but watered-down evangelistic sermon or invitation, on raising their hand and coming forward at an evangelistic meeting, or on mindlessly reciting a 'sinner's prayer' from the back of a tract. They know little conviction of sin and have never seen their need as a lost sinner before God. They claim forgiveness without repentance. Their supposed 'new heart' results in an unchanged life. Their outwardly religious lives or their worldly lives reveal that Christ has not become their Savior and Lord. They are strangers to a personal, experiential acquaintance with Jesus Christ as their prophet, priest, and king. They do not truly fear God, hate sin, love Christ, and pursue holiness.

False assurance generally leads a person into one of two dead ends – the dead end of sentimental emotion or the dead end of dry intellectualism. Living in either of these false gospel cul-de-sacs often results in the rejection of the true gospel that connects the whole man with the gospel – head, heart, and hands. People with false assurance are commonly very hard to reach with the gospel. We fear that tens of thousands who consider themselves to be Christians will wake up in hell to their eternal horror. How dreadful it will be to be self-deceived on the judgment day! No one will enter heaven on that day on false grounds. Many who claim various things they have said or done for Christ, will be told on that day that Christ has never known them savingly (Matt. 7:21-3). Unsound doctrine and godless living will slay their tens of thousands!

One of the problems with people who base their salvation on presumption and easy-believism is that they seldom, if ever, examine whether their faith is genuine and well-founded. Their error could perhaps better be called 'easy assurance-ism' than easy believism. They claim assurance without having a foundation for it. Errors about how one comes to assurance can easily lead to false assurance. A right understanding of assurance helps us avoid such presumption.

A false view can also hinder us from having assurance when we should. Some genuine children of God do not believe they are children of God. They embrace a kind of 'hard believism', looking for evidences that they have no right to expect. Often they look more at themselves and their works than at Christ and the promises of God. There may be solid, biblical evidence that they are children of God, but they are not satisfied with that. They are their own greatest obstacles in attaining assurance. In this case, too, a proper understanding of assurance of faith is important.

Those who have a proper understanding of assurance will avoid both 'easy' and 'hard' believism. On the one hand, assurance will not be regarded as an easy, automatic benefit. They will not be assured of their faith without solid, biblical evidence of faith operating in their lives. They will be aware of the danger of easy believism and will regularly examine or test their hearts and lives by the Word of God. On the other hand, instructed by the Word, they will recognize the evidence of the new birth in their lives and acknowledge its reality. When they have a genuine longing for God and a corresponding hatred for sin, they will acknowledge that these things are worked by the Holy Spirit in them and be comforted by them. They will not despise true, albeit small, marks of grace (Zech. 4:10). It is critical that our assurance can pass the test of soundness of faith and life, even if we have only small measures of the marks of grace that the Bible identifies as the fruit of the Spirit in the saved (Gal. 5:22, 23).

Peace with God and Joy in God

Assurance is inseparable from the peace and comfort of the gospel. Assurance that we are justified from all sin through Christ is necessary if we are to experience peace and joy and hope (Rom. 5:1-3). To experience true peace and joy in the Lord greatly enriches our lives while we are on this earth. That is one reason why Thomas Brooks (1608–1680) titled his book on assurance *Heaven on Earth*.[2] Assurance is related to the peace, comfort, and joy of the gospel and ought to be cultivated.[3]

What peace, security, and joy belong to us when we can sing through all the joys and sorrows of life, 'This mighty God forever lives, our God and Saviour to abide' (cf. Ps. 48:14); when we can call on God in truth as 'our Father' whom we love 'because He first

---

2) Thomas Brooks, *Heaven on Earth: A Christian Treatise on Assurance* (London: Banner of Truth Trust, 1961).

3) J. C. Ryle, *Holiness* (Welwyn Garden City, England: Evangelical Press, 2014), 148–51.

loved us'; when we can hold sweet communion with Jesus Christ as our Savior and Elder Brother and be confident that we know He will soon come again to take us to Himself to glory; when we can be patient in sufferings because we know that they are short and our joys are eternal! Surely, no one on earth can have so much happiness as the Christian who has a well-grounded certainty that the triune God is his salvation, and that 'to live is Christ, and to die is gain' (Phil. 1:21).[4]

That does not mean that Christians will not have times of sorrow over sin, difficulties, and doubts. But Scripture is abundantly clear that Christians ought to exhibit great peace and great joy in the Lord (Neh. 8:10; Phil. 4:7; Heb. 10:19-25). Even in sorrow, we should always be rejoicing. To do that, we must be fully assured of our faith. Charles Spurgeon said of such believers: 'A fully assured Christian is a very giant in our Israel; for happiness and beauty he standeth like Saul, head and shoulders taller than the rest; while for strength and courage he can match with David.'[5]

Christian Service

An assured Christian is an active Christian. Paul said of the Thessalonians, 'For our gospel came not unto you in word only, but also in power, and in the Holy Ghost, and in much assurance' (1 Thess. 1:5). The preaching of the gospel was so blessed in Thessalonica that there was much assurance – both in Paul and in his hearers. Paul goes on to say, 'So that ye were ensamples to all that believe in Macedonia and Achaia. For from you sounded out the word of the Lord not only in Macedonia and Achaia, but also in every place your faith to God-ward is spread abroad; so that we need not to speak any thing' (vv. 7, 8). How amazing! The Thessalonians, newly converted, sounded out the Word of God – that is, they evangelized – so that

---

4) Thomas Jones, *The True Christian; or, The Way to Have Assurance of Eternal Salvation* (London: R. B. Seeley and W. Burnside, 1834), 4–5.

5) Charles Spurgeon, *Metropolitan Tabernacle Pulpit* (Pasadena, Tex.: Pilgrim Publications, 1973), 7 (1861):549.

when Paul journeyed further on, from Thessaly into Macedonia and Greece, he discovered that the Word of God had already come there. These people were so zealous for God because, for one thing, they were assured of their salvation.

A Christian without assurance is seldom concerned about good works. Rather, his spiritual energy is consumed by questioning whether he is saved or not. When that question is not resolved, the person halfheartedly helps others in the service of the Lord. The Puritan Thomas Goodwin said that a Christian who has full assurance of faith is ten times more active than one who does not![6] And J. C. Ryle stated, 'A believer who lacks an assured hope, will spend much of his time in inward searchings of heart about his own state. Like a nervous, hypochondriacal person, he will be full of his own ailments, his own doubtings and questionings, his own conflicts and corruptions. In short, you will often find that he is so taken up with his internal welfare that he has little leisure for other things, and little time for the work of God.'[7]

Some people think that our business here on earth is only to find salvation; once we are saved we have little more to do until we get to heaven. Conversion is viewed as an end in itself. But that is not the case. We are converted for some very important ends or purposes: to be conformed to Christ and to worship and serve God in order to show forth His praise. Romans 8:29 tells us that God's people are predestinated 'to be conformed to the image of his Son'. And 1 Peter 2:9 tells us: 'Ye are a chosen generation, a royal priesthood, an holy nation, a peculiar people; that ye should shew forth the praises of him who hath called you out of darkness into his marvellous light.' God converts us so that we may be made more like His Son and that we may show forth His praise, so that He may be glorified in us.

---

6) Thomas Goodwin, *The Works of Thomas Goodwin* (Grand Rapids: Reformation Heritage Books, 2006), 1:251.

7) J. C. Ryle, *Holiness: Its Nature, Hindrances, Difficulties, and Roots* (Cambridge, England: J. Clarke, 1956), 32.

Communion with God

Assurance is valuable because it enriches our communion with God. How can a person have close communion with God when he is uncertain as to where he stands with God? How difficult would it be for a parent to have a close relationship with a child who is unsure of the love of his father? The child never relaxes and accepts expressions of love. In such an atmosphere, a close relationship is impossible.

By contrast, consider the assurance described in the Song of Solomon when the bride says of her husband, 'My beloved is mine, and I am his' (2:16). There is communion here, fellowship, a warm and trusting relationship, love and confidence on the part of the bride that the love between them is mutual. That is the kind of fellowship that the Lord holds out to His people. He often describes His relationship to them in the closest of terms: Father and child, Husband and wife, Bridegroom and bride, Head and body, and a Friend among friends. The Lord uses the most intimate relationships in life to describe the relationship that He wants with His people. Assurance is necessary to realize that kind of relationship.

Holiness to the Lord

Assurance is critical because it makes a person more holy. Speaking of the assurance that flows out of knowing that we are adopted sons of the Father, John says, 'Every man that hath this hope in him purifieth himself, even as he is pure' (1 John 3:3).

Assurance that does not lead to a more holy walk is false assurance. The person whose assurance is well-founded, who experiences true peace and joy, who is busy in the Lord's service and lives in close fellowship with Him, will lead a holy life. A believer cannot persist in high levels of assurance while he continues in low levels of holiness.

Assurance brings us into close contact with God's power. When we have a trusting relationship with God and confidence in His mercy and grace, our hearts are inflamed with love for God. This love kindles the will and desire to live a holy life. The closer we are to God, the more love we will feel for God and the more holy our lives will be. A holy person is driven by love to God, for Christ's sake. The love of Christ constrains the holy man (2 Cor. 5:14).

Need for Revival

Assurance of faith is sorely needed today because assurance cannot be separated from genuine revival. What is a revival but large numbers of persons coming into the knowledge of Christ and assurance of grace and salvation through Him?

How true that was of Martin Luther! Read Luther on Galatians. Did he not burn with indignation for the way the church of his day left people uncertain about salvation? By contrast, Luther was filled with the assurance that flows out of the gospel. Search his writings and you will feel the power of what he is saying.

Countering Secularization

Assurance is necessary if we are to be God-honoring Christians in a day of great secularization and apostasy. The gospel has always been difficult to live out in the world. But sometimes opposition to the gospel is especially intense. We are living in such a time. We are living in a bruising time.

We are called to be lights on the lampstand in a day of great darkness, while the devil promotes apostasy on all sides, especially within the church and in our educational institutions. To be lights in such darkness we need much assurance.

One of the best ways to counteract secularization as Christians is to let our light shine with the gifts of peace and joy flowing out of assurance because we are exhibits of the gospel. In Philippians 2:15, Paul's prayer is, 'That ye may be blameless and harmless, the sons of God, without rebuke, in the midst of a crooked and perverse nation, among whom ye shine as lights in the world.' Surely one way that a Christian can shine like a light in this evil world is by living in peace and joy. What idea will the world have about God if God's people don't show that it is a wonderful thing to serve the Lord? The psalmist commands us to 'give thanks unto the LORD, for he is good: for his mercy endureth for ever. Let the redeemed of the LORD say so, whom he hath redeemed from the hand of the enemy' (Ps. 107:1, 2). What does it say about God if people cannot detect in us the quiet peace and genuine happiness that sets us apart as His children?

Promotion of Biblical Doctrine

The doctrine of assurance is sorely needed today because doctrine itself is largely despised. Few understand Martin Luther's assertion: 'Doctrine is heaven.' Assurance is the nerve center of doctrine put in *use*, as the Puritans would say; that is, God's truth applied to our own lives and to the life of the world. Assurance entwines itself with the work of the Spirit in every link of the chain of salvation, from effectual calling to glorification. It is inseparable from the doctrines of sin, grace, atonement, and union with Christ. It is conjoined with the marks and steps of grace. It touches on the issue of divine sovereignty and human responsibility; is intimately connected with Holy Scripture; and flows out of election, the promises of God, and the covenant of grace. It is fortified by preaching, the sacraments, and prayer. Assurance is broad in scope, profound in depth, and glorious in height.

Conclusion

How important this whole question of assurance is! It is possible to be saved without assurance, but it is scarcely possible to be a healthy Christian without assurance. You may object: 'Doesn't Scripture affirm that God has a special concern for the poor and needy sinner?' Even the most assured child of God is still a poor and needy sinner. If he ever stops being poor and needy in himself, there is reason to doubt whether his assurance is based on solid ground. Christ must increase and he must decrease (John 3:30).

The Lord is near to those who have a broken heart and a contrite spirit and sigh for assurance. But it does not follow that to remain forever in such a condition is desirable. If we lack assurance, we should seek it diligently, by the light of God's Word, and with the help of His Spirit.

Assurance is vital for our spiritual well-being. Some people think assurance indicates superficiality. In their eyes, one is almost suspect if he has assurance. In reality, those who see doubting and fearing as a sign of deep religious experience, and prefer to press on toward God and glory without assurance, have only a superficial understanding of Scripture. A deeper understanding of gospel truth leads us to recognize the work of the Spirit in our hearts, to acknowledge and rejoice in it, and all the more, to rest with childlike faith in the Lord Jesus Christ.

❧ 2 ❧

Why Do Many Christians Lack Assurance?

Despite its importance, many Christians lack assurance. Some professing Christians think they have it when their lives show they do not; their presumption paves the road to hell for them. They express little, if any, doubt about their salvation while showing little, if any, marks of true Christianity. When they say that they never wrestle with assurance, they mean what they say. I have often been perplexed and amazed by the conversations that I've had with professing Christians who will strongly affirm that they possess assurance of salvation and yet show no interest in the Word, in personal holiness, or in living Christ-centered lives.

Other people say they long to have assurance, but can't ever seem to find or embrace it. Perhaps you are one of those people. The question of assurance is a painfully personal one to you. You can't count the number of times you have said to yourself, to God, and to others: 'Do I love the Lord or not; am I His or am I not?' You have struggled with assurance for years – even decades – and feel no further ahead in your quest than where you were years ago.

I want you to know that I wrote this book especially for you. I feel your pain; I have counseled hundreds of people in the last forty-plus years in your condition. I pray to God that this book is a means He will use to deliver you from the 'lack-of-assurance' bondage that has plagued you. Pray over each chapter you read and stick with me to the end of this book.

In this chapter, I want to examine eleven problems or reasons many true believers who love and serve the Lord may lack assurance. There are many more reasons, no doubt, but these are the major ones. If you are a true believer and you can work through these problems in your mind, you should be well on your way to having at least some degree of assurance.

Our History and Present Experience of Sin

The first reason why we sometimes lack assurance as Christians is sin – sin both past and present. On the one hand, if we have grown up without being conscious of a day when we did not love God and His Son, we still struggle at times with our past and present wickedness. Increasingly we learn that we have so much internal evil in our mind and heart that we can wonder not so much if we love God, but does He really love us when we have such a tendency to sin?

On the other hand, if we have grown up without loving God, we can by stymied in our assurance by the burden of having lived in sin for so long as strangers to God and His grace. We've lived as haters of God; we've dwelt in spiritual darkness and ignorance of the true character of God; we've been spiritually dead so that we do not recognize the beauty of His creative and re-creative handiwork as the God of salvation.

Then all of this changed. By the preaching of the gospel, the Holy Spirit did His amazing work, so that we came to hate sin, to love God, and to pursue holiness. Where once there was enmity, now there is friendship and family. Where hatred ruled, now love is the focus. Where ignorance of God kept us in the dark, now the light has dawned and we begin to see Him as He is. We've been delivered from our spiritual deadness into the glorious life and light of Christ. We've been set free from the powers of darkness that have long enslaved us. And that is all wonderful! Yet, we are prone to stop and look back at our past sinfulness, as well as our present struggles with sin, and say, 'That I can love the lovable God is understandable, for He is altogether lovely in Christ. But can God truly love me when I have such a bad heart and such a bad record of sinning? Can I truly be His child and still be such a sinful person? If I am a true believer, how can I still be drawn to secret sins and so prone to love the world? "O wretched man that I am!" (Rom. 7:24). I've failed so miserably again and again, so how can I be sure that I am truly a redeemed child of God?'

False Conceptions of God's Character and of His Gospel

Second, some believers do not have assurance of faith because they do not have a biblical understanding of God. The heart of a well-founded assurance of faith is, as Paul points out in Romans 8:31-9, a biblical understanding of who God is. Romans 8:31, 32 says, 'What shall we then say to these things? If God be for us, who can be against us? He that spared not his own Son, but delivered him up for us all, how shall he not with him also freely give us all things?'

The anchor of Paul's assurance is, knowing that *God is for us*. He sent His Son into the world to die for us. Paul goes on to say, 'Who shall lay any thing to the charge of God's elect? It is God that justifieth. Who is he that condemneth? It is Christ that died, yea rather, that is risen again, who is even at the right hand of God, who also maketh intercession for us. Who shall separate us from the love of Christ?' (vv. 33-5a).

Paul's understanding of God, who He is, what He has done for us, and why, is the center of his assurance. It is God that justifies; and Christ who died and rose again for us, ascended into heaven and now makes intercession for us – 'who shall separate us from the love of Christ?' Notice that Paul is not saying, 'I am persuaded of God's love because of something inside of me.' He is persuaded that nothing can separate him from the love of Christ – not because he is so sure that he is a child of God, but rather, the other way around: he is sure that he is a child of God because of what he knows about the love of Christ. The center of his thinking is not Paul or anything in himself; it is God! It is Paul's concept of God that gives rise to his assurance.

You may remember in *Pilgrim's Progress* how the burden fell from Christian's back at the cross. God's love for sinners is most clearly displayed at the cross. Too many Christians don't truly believe that. They don't believe that God, like the father of the prodigal son, eagerly looks for His wayward, disobedient children to come home. They don't believe that they are welcome to come to God and be freely forgiven of all their sins. Too many view God the same way as the servant in the Parable of the Talents who said about his lord, 'I knew thee that thou art a hard man' (Matt. 23:24). Too many see God as capricious and harsh. But God commends His love to us 'in that while we were yet sinners, Christ died for us' (Rom. 5:8). When we see His love in the breaking of Christ's body and the shedding of His precious blood, then we have grounds for real assurance, for then we see that the heart of God is yearning for sinners. We see that He is willing to pay the supreme sacrifice to save. Then we believe that God means what He says, 'Look unto me, and be ye saved' (Isa. 45:22), and we affirm with Paul that we are persuaded that nothing shall separate us from the love of God that is in Christ Jesus our Lord (cf. Rom. 8:38-9).

God loves to assure His people that they are His children and He is their Father. What would you think of an earthly father who kept his son and daughter in doubt for many years as to whether he was their real father? Do you think the heavenly Father feels differently about His children? 'What man is there of you, whom if his son ask bread, will he give him a stone? Or if he ask a fish, will he give him a serpent? If ye then, being evil, know how to give good gifts unto your children, how much more shall your Father which is in heaven give good things to them that ask him?' (Matt. 7:9-11).

Doubting believer, understanding who God is in Christ will give a huge boost to your assurance. Read Ephesians 1. Read the Parable of the Prodigal Son (Luke 15:11-24) – or should we call it the Parable of the Loving Father? – and can you honestly say that the heavenly Father does not want to assure His children that they are His? The heavenly Father does not give assurance to His child with a medicine dropper, one drip at a time, but delights to pour it out with an open bottle. He delights in mercy (Micah 7:18) and in giving assurance (Eph. 1:17). Praise God that He is true, faithful, merciful, assuring, and loving in Christ Jesus, and ask God to show that to you.

Lack of Clarity on Justification by Faith

The third reason many believers lack assurance of faith is that they lack clarity on the doctrine of justification by faith alone, often confusing it with sanctification. Justification is clearly spelled out in the Word of God in Romans 4:5: 'To him that worketh not, but believeth on him that justifieth the ungodly, his faith is counted for righteousness', and in Galatians 2:16, 'Knowing that a man is not justified by the works of the law, but by the faith of Jesus Christ.'

Many do not understand that the Lord freely gives to those who ask of Him the results or benefits of all that Christ did on the cross (His passive obedience) and of His life of perfect obedience to the law (His active obedience). By this twofold obedience on behalf of sinners, God's justice is satisfied. He thus may be just and the justifier of those who believe in Jesus (Rom. 3:26).

We can do nothing that will make us worthy or fit to receive God's forgiveness. Nothing is necessary to make us acceptable to God. As poor sinners, we receive the gift of salvation by true faith and are justified; that is, we begin as Christians in a right relationship with the Lord. There is nothing that we can do to make ourselves acceptable to God. God does not justify us because of our sincere sorrow for sin, our good works, or anything else. Justification by faith alone means that all our sins are forgiven only because of what Christ has done.

If we base our justification on some condition that we must fulfill or a particular experience that we must have, we inject a kind of legalism into our justification that destroys its gracious character and robs us of its saving and assuring character. Then our spiritual deficiencies can lead us to spiritual depression, for justification by works, no matter how subtle its form, will demolish assurance. If salvation were by works, we could never do enough of them to be saved! If salvation were by experience, no experience would stand up for long under close scrutiny. Donald Macleod points out that 'there is a very real danger of what is called, paradoxically, evangelical legalism – the view that justification is grounded upon religious experience considered as in itself meritorious'. Faith itself is not the ground of our justification, but only an instrument, a means by which to lay hold of Christ and His righteousness. Faith, Macleod concludes, is neither 'the ground of our justification nor its meritorious cause. We are justified because of the objective and completed righteousness of Jesus Christ. Faith is our grasp of that righteousness. It unites us to Christ. But it is not our rock. If it were, then its every inadequacy, every defect, every crack, would make us tremble.'[1]

It is true that God expects His justified people to put off their sins and do good works, but only as the fruit of being justified, not as a means to being justified. The Belgic Confession of Faith says that when Christians have received Christ by faith as 'the only Savior, they avoid sin, follow after righteousness, love the true God and their neighbor, neither turn aside to the right or left, and crucify the flesh with the works thereof' (Art. 29). But we must remember that none of these things can be the ground of our acceptance with God. Judged in themselves, our best works must fall short, for whatever we do is stained with sin. James says that if we are guilty of breaking the law at one point, we are guilty of breaking the whole law (James 3:2).

Thus, no true Christian will ever feel that he is fit to be accepted by God. Even the holiest of men are accepted by God only because the merits of Christ are imputed to them. Once we understand and believe that, we are released from bondage. We may then go to God as sinners, knowing that God does not require anything from us as a condition for receiving His grace. We may come as we are, resting completely and exclusively on Christ's merits.

This view of justification continues to be an important factor in the lives of those who have been assured of their faith. For when they fall into sin, they are reminded that they are unworthy to be

---

1) Donald Macleod, 'Christian Assurance 1', *Banner of Truth*, no. 133 (Oct. 1974): 18–19.

accepted by God and that if God were not willing to receive us as sinners for Christ's sake, there would be no hope for anyone. That is what it means to live out of Christ: to need His forgiving grace every day, to know that there is nothing in us that is acceptable to God, but that He is willing to wash away all our sins for Christ's sake. Justification by faith alone stands in the foreground of the experience of every child of God who has assurance.

Lack of Confessing Christ

Some weak believers are held back from growing in assurance because their lack of confessing Christ openly among their family and friends keeps them in darkness. That can be compounded in the lives of some by their not partaking of the Lord's Supper because they mistakenly think that they cannot do so until they have full assurance of faith.

John repeatedly warns against the dangers of not confessing Christ in his first epistle. He says in 1 John 2:23: 'Whosoever denieth the Son, the same hath not the Father: [but] he that acknowledgeth the Son hath the Father also.' The word 'acknowledgeth' here is translated elsewhere in 1 John as 'confess'. So, when John speaks of acknowledging that Jesus is the Christ he means more than an intellectual belief that Jesus is God. Confession of Christ is more than an intellectual acknowledgment that Jesus is the Christ.

This same truth is also taught in 1 John 4:2, 3: 'Hereby know ye the Spirit of God: every spirit that confesseth that Jesus Christ is come in the flesh is of God: and every spirit that confesseth not that Jesus Christ is come in the flesh is not of God: and this is that spirit of antichrist, whereof ye have heard that it should come; and even now already is it in the world.' Again, 1 John 4:15 says, 'Whosoever shall confess that Jesus is the Son of God, God dwelleth in him, and he in God.'

The problem for weak believers is that when they do not confess Jesus Christ to others, they bring darkness upon their souls. That, in turn, can multiply doubt within them concerning whether they have ever been truly saved.

Disobedience and Backsliding

Some people do not receive assurance of faith because of their disobedience and backsliding. One cannot enjoy high levels of assurance while he persists in disobedience. Falling into and continuing in sin, while resisting God's will for our lives, grieves and quenches the Holy Spirit, thus robbing us of our good hope for assurance. Refusing to engage in biblical self-examination, and neglecting the spiritual disciplines of Bible study, meditation, and prayer – all of these and more can negatively impact our assurance.

This truth must be balanced with the other factors we have already given. If any one factor is left out or receives too much emphasis, assurance becomes problematic. On the one hand, if little emphasis is placed on the love of God and on justification by faith alone, and much emphasis is placed on how we live, problems result, for then the emphasis shifts towards the idea that one must earn God's favor (legalism). On the other hand, if too much emphasis is on the love of God and on justification by faith and not enough on the call to holy living, there is reason to wonder if our faith is true since it is not bearing fruit (dead faith).

Some people see God's grace in the gospel and understand justification by faith, but they are not careful in their Christian walk. They may be true Christians, for none of God's people live exactly as they should, but those who don't watch and pray that they might not enter into temptation – who are sloppy, careless, and lazy in their Christian walk – need not be surprised if they lack assurance; any assurance they have may be only self-deception. 'A lazy spirit is always a losing spirit', wrote Thomas Brooks, for 'a lazy Christian will always lack four things, viz., comfort, contentment, confidence, and assurance.'[2] We all need to ask ourselves: 'Am I sincere in striving to live in accord with God's Word – His gospel and His law? Do I strive to live after or according to the Spirit, setting my mind on the things of the Spirit, as a debtor to Christ and His saving work?' (Rom. 8:4-5, 12).

---

2) Brooks, *Heaven on Earth*, 111.

There is tension here: God's people may be encouraged when they see signs of the fruit of the Holy Spirit's saving work in their hearts, but they will also be all the more conscious of many areas in which they fall short. Thus, the greatest factor in their assurance will be their understanding of God's grace and that He is willing to forgive them fully and freely, for Christ's sake.

Some tender believers fail to understand the continuing presence of indwelling sin in their lives (Rom. 7:14-25). They are prone to lose their assurance when they stumble over their own failures. Their own conscience condemns them, so that conscience holds a veto power over God's promises. They judge themselves more by their feelings than they do by God's Word.

Let's relate this directly to the words of Scripture. On the one hand, Jesus says, 'Him that cometh to me I will in no wise cast out' (John 6:37). Likewise, Paul says he is persuaded that nothing shall separate us from the love of Christ (Rom. 8:38, 39). On the other hand, Christ says, 'If ye love me, keep my commandments' (John 14:15), and John says, 'Hereby we do know that we know him, if we keep his commandments' (1 John 2:3). These are both biblical truths, and assurance usually grows best when we properly emphasize both.

Ignorance of Satisfying Evidences of Grace

Some children of God fail to receive assurance because they do not know how to appreciate the indwelling ministry of the Holy Spirit as the Spirit of adoption. 'Dwelling on the presence of the Spirit of adoption is a great aid to assurance,' writes Sinclair Ferguson, 'and failure to do so brings with it a lowering of the sense of grace that is freely ours in Christ.'[3]

The neglecting or minimizing of the adopting, indwelling Spirit also keeps believers ignorant of what Spirit-worked evidences of grace they should look for in their lives. They would profit immensely

---

3) Sinclair B. Ferguson, 'The Assurance of Salvation', *The Banner of Truth*, no. 186 (Mar. 1979): 8.

from studying the Beatitudes in Matthew 5:3-12 or the fruit of the Spirit in Galatians 5:22, 23. For example, if God says that hungering and thirsting after Christ's righteousness is a sign of Spirit-worked grace (Matt. 5:6), but you do not know that it is a sign of grace, the presence of it in your life will not give you much comfort. Love for the brethren is a sign of Spirit-worked grace (1 John 3:14), but if you do not know that, you will not get much comfort from loving the brethren. Whatever good we find in ourselves must be something worked in us by the Spirit, contrary to what we are by nature, 'for I am prone by nature to hate God and my neighbor' (Heidelberg Catechism, Q. 5).

William Guthrie (1620–1665), author of the classic *The Christian's Great Interest*, one of the best works on assurance, stressed that some Christians don't seriously search the Scriptures to inquire what evidences of grace provide adequate evidence to our conscience that we are children of God. He then went on to say that the Lord doesn't leave us in the dark here, but clearly and frequently teaches the true evidences and marks of a saving interest in Christ (such as 1 John 1:4; 5:10; 5:13), so that no one is excusable for not knowing such basic evidences.[4]

Guthrie was right. God has given so much Scripture about the marks, fruits, and evidences of a saving relationship with Him that we ought to be able, with the indwelling Spirit's assistance, to discern our state before God. That is not to say that the discernment of our state will always be clear. But, for the most part, we can and should know where we stand with God. The reason that some do not have such assurance is that they do not know the marks and fruits of true conversion.

Possessing a Doubting or Negative Disposition

Some Christians are prevented from embracing personal assurance of salvation because of their own personal disposition. Our natural

---

4) William Guthrie, *The Christian's Great Interest* (London: Banner of Truth Trust, 1969), 33.

temperament and damaged mindset can hinder our assurance. The way that our personalities are 'wired', the way our emotions tip quickly one way or another, and the way that we can be up one minute and down the next can threaten our assurance. Bunyan wrote about a Mr Fearing in Part II of his *Pilgrim's Progress*, who, happily, would never turn back to the world; but he also had a very difficult time embracing any substantial degree of assurance. I had a God-fearing grandfather with this difficulty. He often struggled with whether he should partake of the Lord's Supper, though in the end, he always did, as he could not deny altogether God's work within him. But his level of assurance never seemed to reach a high range. It was obvious to everyone but himself that he was a child of God. Ministers and elders were always trying to encourage him, but sadly, I think doubting just became a way of life for him. Some people naturally doubt and are prone to think negatively. For them, the glass is always half empty, never half full; assurance of faith can seem too good to be true.

Like Mr Fearing, they are full of fears. Though God-fearing, they fear that God's favorable presence is not with them, that they are not included in His electing grace, and that the Lord has not yet begun to work savingly in them. Thinking that their conversion is more their own work than the Lord's work, they tremble at the thought that their conversion doesn't measure up to the typical accounts of conversion they hear from others. They fear that they have sinned too much or are too old and too hardened for the Lord to save. They fear that their faith, hope, and love are of their own making and not from God. They fear that their remaining infirmities will get the best of them: their lack of sanctification, their deficiency in performing spiritual duties, their shallow experience of conviction of sin, their unfruitfulness and worldliness and lukewarmness. They fear temptation will lead them to apostasy and ultimate ruin, that they are too unspiritual and too unworthy to attend the Lord's Supper, and that they will die before they find spiritual liberty and assurance.

One's experiences and background can play a major role in this plethora of fears. Sometimes it may be a problem of having had a preacher who was imbalanced in his preaching, stressing continual self-examination and demands of the law and the holiness of God at the expense of preaching fully about God's grace in Christ, such that he discouraged anyone having assurance in subtle or even direct ways from the pulpit. Such preachers do the opposite of what Robert Murray M'Cheyne advised, which was for preachers to stress that though self-examination is essential, people should take ten looks at Christ for every look they take inside themselves.[5]

Sometimes it is related to having lived for many years with a deeply respected, God-fearing but doubting parent who could never quite attain to assurance of faith. Sometimes it is the distrust endemic to one's personal family or church family; sometimes it is a personal history of abuse at the hands of hypocritical church leaders or parents, with internalized self-hatred as a result; sometimes it's legalism, the works righteousness that has been driven into the mind over and over, and has yet to be purged from one's mind and heart.

Conversion in Early Childhood or Gradual Conversion

Some who struggle with assurance were converted at such a young age or else so gradually as an older child or teenager that they can scarcely pinpoint even an approximate time when they first began to hate sin and love Christ. Someone who is brought from death to life and darkness to light in a sudden conversion experience is often not as troubled with assurance as those whose entrance into saving faith is more gradual and almost imperceptible. It is actually a wonderful blessing to fear the Lord in truth from early childhood, so as to be spared from a time of rebellion spent in worldly ways. True believers whose sin has led them into the world prior to their conversion are often jealous of those converted in early childhood, just as those converted in early childhood are often jealous of those who can more closely pinpoint the time when God brought them from darkness to light. One of the difficulties associated with that

---

5) Andrew Bonar, ed., *Memoir and Remains of the Rev. Robert Murray M'Cheyne* (Edinburgh, 1894), 293.

blessed way of coming to faith early in life is that there is not such a stark contrast in their own experience; hence, they often doubt the genuineness of their conversion, fearing that their love for God and His truth is merely the result of growing up 'under the truth' rather than the fruit of the saving ministry of the Holy Spirit.

You may have come to saving faith in childhood before or later than you think, or even more slowly or more suddenly than you think, but your destination is the most important question. The critical question is: Where are you spiritually today? Do you have faith in Christ alone now for your salvation? Is Christ your all-in-all now?

Looking for the Wrong Kind of Experience

Some children of God suffer from a lack of assurance because, contrary to what the Canons of Dort, Fifth Head, Article 10 states specifically when targeting the Roman Catholic view, they are looking for a 'peculiar revelation contrary to, or independent of the Word of God'. For them, the application of the plain Word of God by faith – which is the King's royal way to assurance that produces by the Spirit's grace the normal conversion experiences of God's children in terms of misery, deliverance, and gratitude (see the *Heidelberg Catechism*) – is somehow insufficient. They can't say how the Word is insufficient, nor can they say clearly just what they are looking for, but from my pastoral experience, their search for some kind of unexplainable, extra-biblical, mystical, special revelation – a kind of Damascus Road voice-from-heaven type of experience like Paul had (Acts 9:1-8) – makes it almost certain that as long as they are looking for such an experience, they will never attain to any substantial degree of assurance; or, in the rare cases of people who think they have experienced it, the fruits do not usually bear out that they have.

This error is not common in many churches today, but in the background of the churches that I have served it was quite common, though not nearly as much today in my own denomination. Nevertheless, it needs to be mentioned here because it does bring many needy, weak believers into great darkness and doubt for lengthy periods of time – sometimes for a lifetime, particularly if one of their parents or grandparents had such experiences and have taught their descendants directly or indirectly that to have anything short of this is to fall short of salvation.

Lack of Acknowledging What God has Done

Some of God's people may know the marks of a saving change, but they are afraid that they don't possess those marks in sufficient strength and clarity. For example, one mark of grace is a hatred of and fleeing from sin. Some people may have experienced such aversion to sin, but afterwards their hatred of sin and holy warfare against it have become weak. Or else they fear that they have sinned too much, that old sins seem to be resurrected far too easily, that they can't begin to compare with other saints they know who seem to conquer sin so much more easily than they can, or that they have never experienced conviction of sin to the depth they think they should to be genuinely converted. They then conclude that their souls are not right with God. They are not willing to acknowledge God's work in them unless it meets their own requirements and expectations.

But God works conviction of sin to different degrees and in different ways in His children. Some experience profound conviction of sin for a year or more before being set free in Christ. Others experience just enough conviction to make them hunger for Christ's righteousness so as to need Him as Savior and Lord, and then experience much more conviction later on, after being converted. When someone once asked the Puritan John Owen how much conviction of sin was needed for a sinner to come to Christ, Owen replied that just enough was needed so that the sinner would come to Christ.

It must be noted that many sinners have come under conviction of sin – even intense and deep conviction – but have not come to Christ. Think of Esau and Judas Iscariot! The question you need to ask is: Have I, by God's grace, through faith and repentance, come to Christ for salvation, and have I found that salvation in Him alone? The Scriptures are clear: 'He that hath the Son hath life; and he that hath not the Son of God hath not life' (1 John 5:12).

In his comprehensive book on assurance, Thomas Brooks pictured the heart of man as a courtroom – the old nature on one side, the new nature on the other. The old nature is the result of Satan's work, and the new nature the result of God's work. Brooks said that some Christians take the side of the old nature, trying to prove that the new nature doesn't exist or is not truly part of God's work. Brooks wrote:

> Let me tell thee, it is thy wisdom and thy duty to remember the command of God that doth prohibit thee from bearing false witness against thy neighbor. That same command doth enjoin thee not to bear false witness against the work of grace upon thine own heart, against the precious and glorious things that God hath done for thy soul. How dare you bear false witness against your own soul and the gracious work of God upon thee? If this be not the way to keep off assurance and to keep thy soul in darkness, I know nothing.[6]

Brooks's point is that there are good signs and bad signs in every true believer's life. It is wrong to acknowledge only the bad signs while failing to acknowledge the good things that the Lord has done in our hearts and in our lives – especially His drawing and driving us to His Son for salvation.

Being Attacked by Satan

Finally, Satan figures prominently in all of the above. His goal is to influence us to fear we have sinned too much for God to save, to retain erroneous views of God and His gospel, to misunderstand the doctrine of justification by faith alone, to shy away from confessing Christ, to enlarge our disobedience and backsliding, to remain ignorant of Scripture's clear teaching on the evidences and marks of saving grace, to possess a doubting or negative disposition, to be discontent without a dramatic conversion, to look for the wrong kind of experience, and to refuse to acknowledge God's saving work in our lives.

---

6) Brooks, *Heaven on Earth*, 42.

Moreover, Satan also strives to keep us in spiritual darkness about our salvation by flooding our minds with doubts and fears. He hurls his fiery darts at us, condemning us, insinuating doubt and suspicion about the sufficiency of Christ's righteousness or the sincerity of our own faith. With insidious methods, he assaults the mind that has neglected to put on the helmet of salvation and fails to hold up the shield of faith, and has forgotten the belt of truth, the breastplate of righteousness, and shoes of the gospel of peace. He taunts us with how sinful we still are and seeks to persuade us that we cannot therefore be children of God.

Thomas Goodwin stressed that Satan's peculiar design and malicious desire is to vex and molest the saints with the temptation to believe that 'God is not their God'. With a variety of devices, Satan strives to undermine our faith, persuading us to doubt our possession of eternal life in Christ and thereby call God a liar. He will use our severe afflictions, erroneous doctrine, false teachers, and a host of other things – particularly our own sins and guilt – to shake, and diminish our assurance and move us to despair of God's mercy or of being loved and chosen by Him. He is, after all, the accuser of the brethren.[7]

Satan works as well through human agents to drive us to despair and crush the least bit of faith or assurance in us. 'Many there be which say of my soul, There is no help for him in God' (Ps. 3:2). 'My tears have been my meat day and night, while they continually say unto me, Where is thy God?' (Ps. 42:3).

Conclusion

Are you having trouble with assurance? I exhort you to examine yourself according to what is written in this chapter. Do not rest in the pious cliché, 'God has to give it to me.' God must give assurance to you, no doubt, but He has also shown that He is willing to give it to all who ask it of Him. And He has revealed how He gives it. And that is through right thinking, the use of our own minds as we

---

7) Goodwin, *Works*, 3:256.

prayerfully meditate upon and appropriate His promises, examining our lives by the marks that He has given us in His Word. As the Puritans were fond of emphasizing, we need a Word-guided, Spirit-assisted self-examination that arrives at a conclusion, yes or no. Too much or too little self-examination arrives at no safe conclusion. It stops short of certainty, and leaves us in despair, or with a mere 'perhaps' or 'maybe'. It can also lead to self-deception and carnal presumption. We should never be satisfied with a 'perhaps' or with any kind of presumption. Looking to Christ and leaning on the Holy Spirit, 'make your calling and election sure' (2 Peter 1:10).

❦ 3 ❦

Is Assurance of Faith
Biblical and Normative?

True Christians yearn for divine affirmation that they are saved
in and by Christ. They want to know, as Paul puts it in Romans
8:14-16, that they *are* the sons of God' and that they *are* the
children of God' (emphasis added) – not that they *may be* the sons
of God now or they *shall* one day, hopefully, be the children of
God. Paul's present-tense verbs impress the mind and heart of the
great abiding certainty that we are truly children of God.

This assurance belongs to the body of Christ. It is not reserved
for a select few who happen to be more spiritually minded than
others. Assurance of faith is biblical and normative for true believers
– at least to some degree. It can be stronger or weaker, but believers
ought to know at least some measure of it.

There is a direct proportionality between faith and assurance.
Strong faith tends to embrace strong assurance and weak faith
tends to embrace weak assurance. In this chapter I want to
show you that saving faith and assurance are closely intertwined
throughout Scripture. I will set the doctrine of assurance of faith
in the flow of the history of redemption, moving progressively
through the Old Testament and then through the New Testament.
In subsequent chapters, I will then show how our forefathers

taught that assurance of faith is to be attained and cultivated on these biblical grounds.[1]

Scriptural Development of Assurance of Faith

All Scripture affirms that assurance is rooted in faith that receives God's gracious redemption in Christ and rests in His word of promise. True assurance is rooted in the truth and trustworthiness of God's Word (Rom. 15:4), the exercises of faith (Heb. 11:1), application of promises (2 Cor. 7:1), discernment of inward evidences (1 John), and the witness of the Spirit (Rom. 8:16) – each of which we will explain in coming chapters – and enables the believer to live in faith and by faith, increasingly indebted to God's grace and thankful for our salvation, living and dying happily in the enjoyment of the comfort that we have in Christ, having peace with God.

Assurance in the Old Testament

Genesis 15:1 records how 'the word of the LORD came unto Abram in a vision, saying, Fear not Abram: I am thy shield, and thy exceeding great reward.' The Lord then gives Abram the twofold promise of a son and a seed or posterity as numerous as the stars in heaven: 'So shall thy seed be.' And Abram 'believed in the LORD; and he counted it to him for righteousness' (v. 6). This text is the first in the Bible that mentions justification by faith alone; Abram is declared righteous because he believes in the Lord. But this was not the starting point of faith for Abram. As the Lord reminds him now (v. 7), at the call of God, Abram ('by faith', Heb. 11:8) set out from Ur of the Chaldees in search of an unknown country. From this beginning, his faith grew in both depth of conviction and scope of vision, until he became 'strong in faith, giving glory to God; and being fully persuaded that, what he had promised, he was able also to perform' (Rom. 4:20, 21).

---

1) Much of this chapter is largely a summary of Robert Letham's helpful thesis, 'The Relationship Between Saving Faith and Assurance of Salvation' (ThM thesis, Westminster Theological Seminary, 1976).

The concept of faith as resting or relying on 'the LORD' (Yahweh or Jehovah, the covenantal name of Israel's God, which signifies His unchangeable and faithful character) runs throughout the entire Old Testament. Depending on the preposition used, faith can refer to trust placed *on* the person of the LORD (Ps. 31:15; Prov. 28:25; Jer. 49:11), *in* Him (2 Kings 18:5; 1 Chron. 5:20; Ps. 143:8; Prov. 16:20; Zeph. 3:2), or directed *to* Him (2 Kings 18:22; Ps. 86:2; Prov. 3:5). Israel's confidence in their covenant God and His redemptive work in covenantal history is of an assuring nature. Saving faith in the Abrahamic covenant was synonymous with knowing, trusting in, and relying upon Israel's faithful covenant-keeping God, assured that He could and would fulfil His promises to His people (Ps. 89:34).

In the prophets, assurance and confidence in God was often future-oriented. The present and immediate future often presented bleak prospects with grim overtones of judgment, but the distant future was one of great hope, for then Jehovah will come to rule the nations and punish the wicked (Isa. 2, 11, 13–25, 46, 47; Jer. 25, 43, 46–51; Ezek. 25–32, 38, 39). Jehovah's coming will usher in a new era in which the promises to the covenant community will be fully realized and their oppression will end. The law of God will be engraved on the hearts of many people (Ezek. 36:22-31) who will come to know the Lord inwardly and will be brought to a new maturity (Jer. 31:31-4); indeed, the whole world will become the beneficiary of the Spirit's sanctifying operations, without distinction of race, sex, or class (Joel 2:28-32). Salvation will come to any who call upon the Lord. The Lord's central covenant promise which sustained His people throughout their history – 'Ye shall be my people, and I will be your God' (Ezek. 36:28) – will reach its culmination in the new age to come.

The Psalms revel in assurance of faith, eliciting confidence in the mercy of a forgiving God who does not forsake or destroy His people even when they fail to trust His saving power (Pss. 78, 106). The psalmists are assured that Jehovah's mercy is everlasting (Ps. 136:1-26) and that His preservation of His people will not cease

(Ps. 121). Individually, too, the psalmists confess with assurance that Jehovah will deliver them personally from sin, death, condemnation, and all kinds of danger (Pss. 1, 34). Jehovah is their portion in life, their deliverer in death, and their source of life and joy eternally (Ps. 16). Despite appalling sorrow at times (Ps. 22), God's covenant love will follow them all the days of their lives and they will be with God forever (Ps. 23:6).

This is not to say, however, that every Old Testament believer always possessed a conscious sense of his own assurance of salvation. Certain portions of the Old Testament, including some of the Psalms, indicate that even some of the most stalwart believers occasionally lacked assurance, felt the absence of divine favor, and feared – even nearly despaired – that God had cast them off. For example, David in Psalms 38 and 42, Asaph in Psalms 73 and 77, and Heman in Psalm 88, all cried out in confusion, asking why God seemed to have withdrawn His favor. In an age where material prosperity was often closely associated with divine benediction, Psalm 73 wrestles with the perplexing problem of the sufferings of the righteous in the face of the prosperity of the wicked: 'Verily I have cleansed my heart in vain' (v. 13). Psalm 88 voices a cry of dereliction from a servant of the Lord undergoing horrific sufferings under the wrath of God and at the hands of wicked men.

Though assurance was not always enjoyed by the Old Covenant believer, the Old Testament as a whole stresses that assurance was the normal experience of the believer, even if it was often only future-oriented. Through all the ups and downs of God's children in the Old Covenant, faith relied upon the promises of the covenant God. In the New Testament, the faith of Old Covenant saints is commended for its assured trust (Heb. 10:39–12:2). Though revelation and redemption are yet in preparatory stages in the Old Testament and assurance is somewhat more obscure than in the New Testament, the Old Testament believer's assurance of the abiding covenant love of Jehovah differs not at all from our understanding today of assurance of faith being rooted in the character and promises of God. As B. B. Warfield wrote:

The reference of faith is accordingly in the Old Testament always distinctly soteriological; its end the Messianic salvation; and its essence a trusting, or rather an entrusting of oneself to the God of salvation, with full assurance of the fulfillment of His gracious purposes and the ultimate realization of His promise of salvation for the people and the individual. Such an attitude towards the God of salvation is identical with the faith of the New Testament, and is not essentially changed by the fuller revelation of God the Redeemer in the person of the promised Messiah.[2]

As the Westminster Confession of Faith (11.6) makes clear, justification by faith (and therefore the Spirit's gift of justifying faith) was 'one and the same' under both Testaments. The privileges granted to the justified under the New Testament are greater, but not their faith or the measure of assurance to which they can attain by faith. The Holy Spirit was active in assuring believers in the Old Testament in all the ways that He is active in the New Testament, though only to some and not to all (cf. Westminster Confession of Faith, 20.1). Continuity is avowed here, but also some novelty; for faith, receiving God's new utterance in the words and deeds of Christ in the New Testament (Heb. 1:1, 2), becomes a fuller assurance of present salvation (cf. Joel 2:28-32 and Acts 2:16-21).

Assurance in the New Testament

In the New Testament, assured faith is also viewed as a normative privilege and blessing. The Synoptic Gospels (Matthew, Mark, and Luke) and Acts present faith as assured and assuring trust in the Messiah who grants forgiveness of sins. The design of the Synoptic Gospels is to establish confidence and assurance in the redemptive facts of Christ's incarnation, ministry, death, and resurrection by showing that the promises of the Old Testament are now being fulfilled. The Promiser and the promises are now present in the person of the Messiah. Faith is now exercised in the incarnate King

---

2) Benjamin B. Warfield, *Biblical Doctrines*, in *The Works of Benjamin B. Warfield* (Grand Rapids: Baker, 1981), 2:489–90.

whose kingdom is here. Faith trusts in the living Messiah who has power to heal soul and body – to forgive sins and to heal from every sickness and disease (Mark 2:5; Matt. 9:28); indeed, all things are possible with Him (Mark 9:23, 24).

The effects of saving faith, presented in the Synoptic Gospels, are astounding: those who have faith the size of a grain of mustard seed can move mountains (Luke 17:6). This implies, as Jesus teaches elsewhere more explicitly, that there are varying degrees of faith (Matt. 8:10; Luke 7:9, 17:5). Matthew teaches us that while Jesus reproved 'little faith' in His disciples and commended 'great faith' in the centurion and the Canaanite woman, He affirmed that any degree of faith in exercise is sufficient for receiving answers to prayer (Matt. 17:20, 8:10, 15:28, 21:22).

In the Book of Acts, the Pentecostal outpouring of the Spirit fulfills the covenant promises and imparts the fullness of assurance (Joel 2:28-32; Acts 2:16-21). Peter can claim that the promise to Abraham of universal blessing through his seed is now being fulfilled by the risen Christ; in Christ, all the families of the earth are being blessed (Acts 3:24-6). There is no room for doubt that Jesus is both Lord and Christ (Acts 2:36). Now faith is even more focused on the person of Christ. Christ's displays of Messianic power in the Synoptic Gospels give way to a fuller revelation in His crucifixion, resurrection, and glorification. Those who have faith are now called believers (2:44, 4:32, 13:39), but the word *faith* is now directed most commonly to the person of Christ (5:14, 9:42, 11:17, 16:31, 18:8, 19:4). Faith in Christ is presented as an assured, forthright commitment to His person, which brings with it salvation both here and now, and hereafter.

The apostle John's writings, especially his Gospel and First Epistle, point to the full communion with Christ that results from the knowing and trusting nature of saving faith. The express purpose of John's Gospel was to promote saving faith in Jesus Christ (20:31). John's emphasis on coming to Jesus in total self-surrender, on believing in Him with full allegiance, and on 'eating and drinking Him' in radical commitment to Him, all point to a fullness of experience that

48

is assuring (John 6:35-58). Faith in Christ provides an assurance of being truly alive, both now and in the world to come, through Christ Himself, the resurrection and the life (John 11:2, 26).

John's First Epistle was written to assure those who have saving faith that they are indeed saved. To do that, John underscores the intimate connection between assurance of salvation and the gift of the Spirit. We are assured of our salvation by the mutual abiding of the Spirit in us and us in Him (3:24, 4:13). That abiding can be known by the good works that flow forth from believers' lives, such as keeping God's commandments (2:3-6; 3:4-10, 22-24; 4:21; 5:3) and loving fellow believers (3:11-18; 4:7-21), as well as by not loving the world and the things it lusts for (2:15-17) and by not living in habitual sin (3:6, 9), but confessing your sins and forsaking them.

Paul's epistles stress that faith is an assured hope based on divine promises that have been fulfilled in Christ. Paul affirms repeatedly that he possesses this assured hope for himself. Nearly every letter opens with Paul declaring that he is a servant of Jesus Christ; he is an apostle who belongs to Christ, and can call Him 'my God' (1 Cor. 1:4). He frequently relates how he was converted and from it draws assurance of his own election and final redemption (Gal. 1:15, 16; 1 Tim. 1:12-17). He fully expects to soon be received into a state of glorification with Christ (Phil. 1:19-25; 2 Tim. 4:7, 8).

Some passages, such as Philippians 3:11-14, 1 Corinthians 4:1-5 and 9:24-7, at first appear to temper Paul's hearty assurance. These passages, however, need to be understood in their context. Philippians 3:11-14 should be understood in the context of Paul's impending trials and the possibility of his receiving a death sentence (Phil. 1:8, 12-25). The uncertainty Paul expressed should therefore be understood in terms of his present earthly life, not of his ultimate salvation. Paul had not yet attained the final perfection of the resurrection, and consequently lacked certainty as to whether he would remain alive or go to be with Christ in preparing for that great event. In 1 Corinthians 4:1-5, Paul was not in doubt of his own salvation, but recognized that, in the context of the final assize, all human verdicts are ultimately prejudgments. This served as one of his arguments against the factional spirit of the Corinthians, who were far too quick to make rash assessments (1:12, 13; 4:6-13). Nor does 1 Corinthians 9:24-7 teach that Paul doubted his own salvation; rather, he was calling the Corinthians to self-examination and watchfulness to keep them from the dangers of apostasy.

Paul built his case for assurance of salvation on several other grounds as well, including:

- the immutable purpose of God in redemption, who predestinates His people to salvation in love (Eph. 1:4, 5);

- the accomplishment of redemption in Christ (Rom. 5:1-11; 2 Cor. 3:7-18);

- the believer's union with Christ by faith (Rom. 5:12-21; 6:1-11; 1 Cor. 6:13-17, 15:12-28; 2 Cor. 4:7-14, 5:14-17; Eph. 1);

- the saving work of the Holy Spirit in applying redemption (Rom. 8; 1 Cor. 12:13; Eph. 1:13, 14; Col. 1:25-8);

- the nature of saving faith as abandonment of all self-merit in fully centering on Christ (Rom. 3:22-6, 4:16-25, 8:20-24, 10:5-13; 2 Cor. 8:5; Gal. 3:21-9); and

- the declarations of God concerning the reward of the faithful, whose good works evidence their saving faith in Christ (2 Cor. 5:10; 2 Tim. 4:7, 8, 14).

Paul's warnings do not negate that most believers possess assurance. The warnings in Romans 14:15 and 1 Corinthians 8:11 against destroying a weaker brother by offending his conscience through an abuse of the principle of Christian liberty deals with the seriousness of sinning against the law of love, not with the loss of assurance. The warning in 1 Corinthians 11:27-32 about partaking of the Lord's Supper unworthily addresses carnal presumption, not true assurance; self-examination is intended to promote assurance, not overthrow it. The warning in 1 Corinthians 10:12 to take heed lest one fall is an exhortation to watchfulness rather than a denial of assurance.

In Hebrews, faith is based upon the excellency and finality of Christ's redemptive work, which surpasses the prophets (1:1-3), angels (1:3-14), Moses (3:1-6), Aaron (5:1-10, 7:1-28), and all the high priests of the Levitical economy (9:1–10:18). All the warning passages in Hebrews are encouragements to persevere in the faith despite numerous difficulties and discouragements; none of them deny perseverance and assurance. The author reminds the Hebrew Christians that though he warns them not to fall into presumption or unbelief, he is persuaded of better things of them (Heb. 6:9). He exhorts them to 'come boldly unto the throne of grace' (Heb. 4:16), and reminds them that they have 'boldness to enter the holiest', that is, God's heavenly dwelling place, 'by the blood of Jesus', and should 'draw near' to God 'with a true heart in full assurance of faith' (Heb. 10:19, 22).

James stresses that faith is antithetical to doubt. Faith is single-mindedness; doubt is double-mindedness (1:5-8). Faith shows its life and reality by producing good works in the believer; faith is thus confirmed or assured by our good works, and is strengthened through enduring trials patiently, for Christ's sake (2:18-26; 1:4, 12).

Peter's epistles show faith as confident hope which brings forth love and joy. Faith is always directed to Christ, looking forward to the final redemption of all things. Meanwhile, the believer is 'kept' or preserved by 'the power of God through faith unto salvation' to receive an indestructible inheritance (1 Peter 1:3-12). Nothing can destroy the assurance of that faith – not even trials or persecutions, which, in fact, help the believer identify with Christ and thereby are God's will for our lives now (4:12-14, 19; cf. Rom. 8:29).

The Second Epistle of Peter stresses that the believer does not gain assurance by looking at himself or anything he has produced apart from God's promises, but by relying on God's all-sufficient provision for 'for life and godliness' in Christ, and resting in His 'exceeding great and precious promises' (2 Peter 1:3, 4). The same promises that lead to salvation are sufficient to lead the believer to assurance. As assurance grows, God's promises become increasingly real and meaningful to the believer.

The New Testament, particularly in its repeated admonitions to seek assurance, also acknowledges the possible lack of assurance in the Christian's life. Peter urges, 'Give diligence to make your calling and election sure' (2 Peter 1:10); by implication, you are falling short if you do not. Paul tells the Corinthians that they should examine themselves as to whether they are in the faith (2 Cor. 13:5), for all is in vain if they are not. The First Epistle of John repeatedly shows how believers may know that they know God (1:7; 2:3, 5, 23, 27; 3:14, 19; 4:13; 5:2, 13), and in Hebrews, the apostle exhorts us to 'draw near with a true heart in full assurance of faith' (10:22), implying that there were those who were experiencing less than full assurance of faith. All of this, however, is not to deny that the roots of assurance lie in saving faith, which, by its very nature, cannot be overcome by doubt. Assurance in both the Old and New Testaments is normative for believers, though not every believer possesses large measures of it.

In sum, the very character of the New Covenant, based on Christ's death and resurrection and the Spirit's indwelling presence, in fulfillment of the promises of God, indicates that assurance must be a constitutive element of saving faith, even if it is only in seed form. Whatever form assurance takes in different stages of redemptive revelation, it appears to coalesce with faith. This is supported by such concepts as the fidelity of God, the truth of His promise, the centrality of Christ and His mediatorial work, the infallible testimony of the Holy Spirit, the radical nature of salvation, and the sovereignty of grace.

Conclusions and Applications on Assurance

Scripture shows that assurance of salvation is the normal possession of Christians in principle, despite varying measures of conscious enjoyment of it. Passages such as Psalm 88 warn us not to deny our redemption if we temporarily lack assurance. Though some degree of assurance for believers is normal, that normativity does not make assurance essential for salvation. The lack of assurance ought to direct us to Scripture's stress on the ministry of the Word, the Spirit, and the sacraments in cultivating assuring faith within the covenantal community of the living church.

Assurance is based on the covenant of grace and is sealed with the blood of Christ. Though assurance remains incomplete in this life, varies in degree, and is often assaulted by affliction and doubt, its riches must never be taken for granted. It is both a gift, for it is always the gracious and sovereign gift of the Triune God, and a pursuit, for it must be diligently sought through the means of grace (2 Peter 1:5-10). It only becomes well-grounded when it evidences fruits and marks of grace such as love of God and His kingdom, filial obedience, godly repentance, hatred of sin, brotherly love, and humble adoration of the triune God. Assurance produces holy living marked by spiritual peace, joyful love, humble gratitude, and cheerful obedience. Happily, these marks and fruits of grace are also the fruit of Christ's redemption received by faith through grace.

So, let me ask you: Do you possess the kind of personal assurance of faith of which Scripture speaks? And if not, why not? Are you unconverted? Are you not at all interested in spiritual things? Are the concerns of this life and the pleasures of this life more important to you? Well, if that is the case you better not have assurance, for you are on your way to eternal perdition. And if things do not change, that is where you will end up. Realize that if you do not turn and seek the Lord, your present desire to be separated from God will be granted to you forever.

Are you perhaps longing for the Lord and have no conscious sense of assurance? Well, if this is your condition, have you repented of your sins before God and believed in Christ alone for salvation? If not, why not? What are you waiting for? You know that Christ offers you salvation. You desire to have that salvation. Trust God to grant it to you; He is more willing to give this miracle of grace than you are willing to receive it. So, why don't you receive it? You can never expect to have assurance before you have faith.

From what we have considered about assurance throughout the Scriptures, it is clear, as the Westminster Confession states (18.3), that it is our duty to sincerely and earnestly seek to attain to large measures of assurance of faith. God does not want to see His people going through life without enjoying the assurance of His love and of their eternal salvation. He wants them to enjoy peace and to rejoice in their salvation through union with Christ (Col. 1:13, 14; 1 John 4:13), to know they are in a sure covenant relationship with the triune God and are adopted by Him into God's family (2 Sam. 23:5; Rom. 8:12-17), to know that they will finally prove victorious in Christ over all enemies (their old nature, sin, death, hell, and the grave) (Rom. 7:24, 25; 1 Cor. 15:51-8), and to know that they have eternal life and that heaven will be their final home (John 10:28; 2 Cor. 5:1).[3] The idea that somehow it is safer to be only an earnest seeker rather than an assured child of God is anathema to the Lord and the testimony of Scripture from Genesis to Revelation. To glorify God and for our own soul's good, let us all seek diligently to obtain a well-founded assurance or to deepen it in our own Christian lives.

---

3) Jones, *The True Christian*, 16–20.

❧ 4 ❧

Three Possibilities
Concerning Assurance

No group of theologians worked harder or were better at spelling out
the biblical doctrine of assurance of faith than did the seventeenth-
century Puritans. They treasured assurance of personal salvation.[1]
They viewed the assurance of peace with God as a fountain that
refreshes the Christian in his trials on the road to glory (Rom. 5:1-5).
Brooks said that assurance makes 'heavy afflictions light, long
afflictions short, bitter afflictions sweet'. It 'makes the soul sing care
away'. It also makes Christian faith 'more motion than notion, more
work than word, more life than lip, more hand than tongue'.[2]

The Puritan doctrine of assurance was formally codified by the
Westminster Confession of Faith in Chapter 18, 'Of the Assurance
of Grace and Salvation' – the first and by far the most important
chapter devoted to assurance in any Reformed confession. It is a

---

1) At least twenty-five members of the Westminster Assembly wrote books
on the doctrines of faith and assurance. For their names, see Joel R. Beeke, 'The
Assurance Debate: Six Key Questions', in *Drawn into Controversie: Reformed
Theological Diversity and Debates within Seventeenth-century British Puritan-
ism*, ed. Michael A. G. Haykin and Mark Jones (Göttingen: Vandenhoeck &
Ruprecht, 2011), 264.

2) Thomas Brooks, *The Works of Thomas Brooks* (Edinburgh: Banner of Truth
Trust, 2002), 2:41; 3:54, 160.

biblical, experiential, pastoral, and practical masterpiece spelled out for us in four short paragraphs. The first paragraph talks about various possibilities we have in relation to assurance. The second paragraph deals with how we get assurance – that is, the grounds upon which assurance is based. The third paragraph addresses how we cultivate and grow in our assurance. And the last paragraph explains how we can lose and then regain our assurance of faith. In several chapters I want to unpack these four paragraphs for you, as I believe there is no better way to explain the basics of assurance of faith than to expound chapter 18 of the Westminster Confession. I will do this primarily by using a lesser-known Puritan writer who I think is one of the best Puritan writers on this subject: Anthony Burgess (d. 1664), who served as a minister of Sutton Coldfield, Warwickshire, England, for more than two decades. Burgess, who was also an important member of the Westminster Assembly, wrote most clearly on assurance of faith in his classic, *Spiritual Refining*.[3]

In this chapter, we will examine the first paragraph of the Westminster Confession's eighteenth chapter, interfacing it with explanations from Burgess's book:

> Although hypocrites, and other unregenerate men, may vainly deceive themselves with false hopes and carnal presumptions of being in the favour of God, and estate of salvation (which hope of theirs shall perish): yet such as truly believe in the Lord Jesus and love Him in sincerity, endeavouring to walk in all good conscience before Him, may,

---

3) Anthony Burgess, *Spiritual Refining: The Anatomy of True and False Conversion; A Treatise of Grace and Assurance wherein are Handled the Doctrine of Assurance, The Use of Signs in Self-Examination, How True Graces may be Distinguished from Counterfeit, Several True Signs of Grace, and Many False Ones* (1662; reprint, Ames, Ia.: International Outreach, 1996), see esp. 1–60 (sermons 1–11) and 670–86 (sermons 116–18). I have edited these fourteen sermons for the modern reader in Anthony Burgess, *Faith Seeking Assurance* (Grand Rapids: Reformation Heritage Books, 2015). For a good summary of Burgess's life and insights into his role in various committees at the Westminster Assembly, including its deliberations on assurance, see Jonathan Master, *A Question of Consensus: The Doctrine of Assurance after the Westminster Confession* (Minneapolis: Fortress Press, 2015), 63–6, 81–139.

in this life, be certainly assured that they are in the state of grace, and may rejoice in the hope of the glory of God, which hope shall never make them ashamed.

The Confession presents three possibilities in relation to assurance: the possibility of false assurance, the possibility of true assurance, and the possibility of a lack of true assurance.

False Assurance

The Confession begins its explanation of the doctrine of assurance by addressing the issue of 'false hopes and carnal presumptions'. Desirous as the Puritans were to lead people into the reality of Christian assurance, they were also deeply concerned not to lead them into the disastrous shortcut of what they called 'false hope' or 'false peace'. Assurance which was not, as they put it, 'soundly bottomed' – that is, not firmly grounded – is not, therefore, an assurance that will stand when the great judgment day of testing comes. False assurance, the Puritans believed, was a real danger. This was one of the ways the deceitfulness of sin and the fallen human heart expresses itself. People are prone to deceive themselves into a false peace, based on an assurance grounded only on their favorable opinion of themselves.

Putting it theologically, the Puritans taught that people are prone to speak peace to themselves when God does not speak peace to them. The Puritans analyzed the reasons for this form of self-deception in considerable detail. They concluded that it is due to the proud temper and propensities that indwelling sin imparts to the human mind and heart in things spiritual. For example, arrogance and conceit about one's own spiritual condition leads to false assurance. My own religiosity, sincerity, conviction of sin, repentance, zeal, morality, and a host of other things that are inherent to me then are viewed by me as the ground – or at least part of the ground – of my peace and salvation, rather than finding the ground of all my peace and salvation in Christ alone. Then there's the obstinacy of the human heart – obstinately believing that because you've attended church faithfully for decades, it's scarcely possible that you are not a

Christian. Unwillingness can also play a major role – unwillingness to take spiritual inventory of one's soul's condition, to rethink the matter, to admit that there might be any reason for doubting one's personal security.

So does ignorance, said the Puritans. If people don't understand the gospel, if they don't know what the new birth, faith, and repentance are, they are in great danger of assuring themselves that they are right with God when they are not. Slothfulness in self-examination and in spiritual matters as habits of the fallen human mind often betrays men into false peace. Due to spiritual drowsiness, they often will not seriously apply to themselves what they hear preached about the new birth, faith, and repentance. They may hear of these things but they won't apply them and they never realize, therefore, that these things, if applied, would expose them. So they go on in their false peace.

Similarly, fallen man is prone to glean false assurance from legalism. He's prone to suppose that since he attends church or practices other Christian duties, he can be assured of his salvation. Many religious people today have the form right – they do all the correct things. They go through all the right motions. They are assured that they are right with God, but it is all false peace and false assurance, the Puritans would say. Any or all of this, and much more, can lead people into a false assurance and anchor them there.

If people in this sad spiritual category are ever to be saved, somehow that false peace must be taken from them, and they must learn to rest their lives on a better foundation than yet they've found. Consequently, the Puritans highlighted the danger of false peace. As sinners, men are prone to it and when they fall into it, it's utterly disastrous and ruinous for their souls. They knew that people are prone to Phariseeism, the quest for a righteousness of one's own, attained by doing the works of the law.

This, then, is how the Puritans saw the problem of false, self-deceiving assurance. On the one hand, they were anxious that men and women coming into faith should also be led into the fullness of assurance. On the other hand, they were anxious that no one should be allowed to remain in a state of false peace. The Puritans sought to lead their congregations between these two extremes of error into true faith and true assurance.

As a typical Puritan, Anthony Burgess stressed that it is a responsibility of great importance for the people of God to be assured that there is a true and saving work of grace in them to distinguish them from hypocrites. There are certain signs of grace by which a man may discern what he is, and where he stands with God.

This involves a practical and experiential knowledge, which is much more than mere head knowledge. There is a great difference between hearing that honey is sweet and tasting its sweetness for yourself. This is what the Bible often means by 'knowing' something – knowledge tested by experience, that is, and not merely notional or theoretical.

It's the difference between seeing a place on a map and going there to see it yourself. It makes our hearts a copy of the Bible, so that all God's promises and warnings have their echo there. This knowledge of holiness makes us dead to all human greatness and worldly delights. It makes the Word and worship sweet to our souls, and helps us to leave behind empty controversies about religion. It gives us the kind of knowledge that produces godly action. It establishes the truth to us in a way that helps us endure persecution rather than let it go.

However, this experiential testing of ourselves faces real obstacles. First, we might approach this question with sinful self-love and self-confidence. 'He that trusteth in his own heart is a fool' (Prov. 28:26). Second, we might look at good actions but ignore the motives. Real godliness is inward, not outward (Rom. 2:28). Third, we might test ourselves by false standards. Instead of the Word of God, the Bible, we might take up what is old, or popular, or traditional for our guide. Fourth, we might confuse good habits or good manners for godliness.

Burgess was deeply convinced of the significance of the Confession's phrase, 'false hopes and carnal presumptions'. In general, there are three kinds of people who take the name of Christians, he said. Some have only the name but no power so that they deny Christ by their works. Others have some influences and operations of the Spirit of God upon them. But they are like embryos that miscarry before the new birth. Their affections are somewhat moved by the truth (Matt. 13:20-22), but the Holy Spirit does not dwell in them as members of the body of Christ. However, some are members of Christ's body, and receive a life-giving influence from Him, as branches do from the vine (John 15:5). The least of believers is far above the best of hypocrites, because he is born again into a true experiential knowledge of Christ's sufferings and resurrection. Someone may have experienced something of the power of spiritual gifts for ministry, the bitterness of sin, a desire for spiritual benefits, an enjoyment of the Word, and a change in their lifestyle – but still be unsaved. The true believer has a different heart (Luke 8:15), for spiritual light dwells in him permanently to make him more holy and dependent on the Lord.

Burgess used some of Jesus's parables, such as the two builders (Matt. 7:24-7) and the ten virgins (Matt. 25:1-13), to show the tragic possibility of people thinking they are saved when they are not, and thereby deceive themselves for eternity.[4] He wrote, 'It is a sad delusion for an ungodly man to be persuaded that his state [for eternity] is good when it is nothing but sin and death. We pity those who are…deluded by the devil appearing as an angel of light.'[5]

Today, varieties of false assurance abound in Christendom. Samplings of these – many of which have some overlap with each other – include:

• *Automatic assurance* teaches that if you believe, assurance is automatic. If you don't have full assurance, you don't have faith. If you have faith, you have full assurance. Automatic assurance often promotes a shallow, easy, false assurance; as John MacArthur writes, it can lead to 'a fatal spiritual apathy. This false assurance is the

---

4) *Faith Seeking Assurance*, 7–8 (*Spiritual Refining*, 3).

5) *Faith Seeking Assurance*, 52 (*Spiritual Refining*, 19).

bane of our age.'[6] Automatic assurance does not bear up under the scrutiny of Scripture; for example, many of the psalms make clear that it is quite possible to have real faith and yet, at the same time, have no or little certainty of having that real faith (Pss. 38, 73, 88).

• *External assurance* is usually assurance that is based on what others say about a person – such as an evangelist, a pastor, or a priest. Too often today, as Paul Washer states:

> The gospel call to repent and believe has been replaced with a call to accept Christ and repeat the sinner's prayer, which is often at the end of tracts and the conclusion of emotional and often manipulative public invitations. Many people no longer obtain assurance of salvation by a careful consideration of their conversion and lifestyle in light of the Scriptures. Rather, it is granted by a well-meaning minister who is quick to pronounce the full benefits of salvation upon any who have prayed to receive Christ with any degree of apparent sincerity.
>
> The result of these drastic alterations in the gospel is that multitudes of individuals demonstrate little evidence of saving grace, yet walk with the greatest assurance of salvation and respond with the greatest offense to anyone who would question their confession. They believe themselves saved, carry their assurance in their heart, and have the affirmation of a religious authority. They have seldom heard a gospel warning to empty confessors of faith or been admonished to examine themselves in light of the Scriptures or test themselves for objective evidences of conversion (Matt. 7:13-27; 2 Cor. 13:5; Titus 1:16). They sense no urgency and find little need to make their calling and election sure (2 Peter 1:10).[7]

The problem with this is that no pastor or anyone else has the right to give assurance to anyone. Only God can give and affirm assurance through His Word, for He alone knows the heart and can confirm that to a person through His Word. First Samuel 16:7 puts it this

---

6) John MacArthur, 'Foreword', in Donald S. Whitney, *How Can I Be Sure I'm a Christian? What the Bible Says About Assurance of Salvation* (Colorado Springs, Colo.: NavPress, 1994), 7.

7) Paul Washer, *Gospel Assurance and Warnings* (Grand Rapids: Reformation Heritage Books, 2014), 3–4.

way, 'The LORD seeth not as man seeth; for man looketh on the outward appearance, but the LORD looketh on the heart.' External faith and assurance are not acceptable to God.

• *Hyper-Calvinistic assurance* is assurance that goes beyond Calvin's teaching (hence, 'hyper-Calvinism'). In hyper-Calvinism assurance can take various forms. One form places the promises of God and faith in the background and the marks of grace and mystical experiences cut loose from Scripture in the foreground. That form teaches that marks of grace must first be seen *before* a sinner is invited and allowed to believe the gospel. Another form of hyper-Calvinism embraces antinomianism (*anti*: against; *nomos*: law; hence, 'against the law') which downplays obedience to the Ten Commandments as well as sanctifying marks and fruits of grace and instead relies primarily on spiritual, mystical experiences for assurance. Instead of stressing, as Jesus does, 'ye shall know them by their fruits' (Matt. 7:16), it implicitly teaches, 'ye shall know them by their spiritual, mystical experiences'.

• *Emotional assurance* gets its assurance out of a frenzied kind of feeling which has no objective basis in the Scriptures. Closely associated with this is *'charismatic assurance'* based on a kind of second blessing, such as speaking in tongues. Nowhere does Scripture commend such emotion-based assurance.

• *Minimalistic assurance* is assurance that easily excuses sin and a lifestyle that doesn't aim to please God. It thrives on excuses and avoids bringing the soul to the bar of God's Word. It says things like this: 'I know I'm sinning; I just find it tough to resist this sin. But don't worry, God will understand and will forgive me. God knows I'm not perfect yet; perhaps I'm just backslidden, but I am sure God will bring me back. After all, He converted me when I was a child. I confessed my sin to Him and He forgave me, so He certainly will not forsake me now.'

Or, 'I know I have sinned and keep on sinning, but I will deal with it later. How can you imply that I might not be saved? That's crazy. Can't you see all that God has blessed me with? I've got a beautiful wife, good kids, a great job, a nice house, and lots of good,

Christian friends. Besides, I never skip church. Look, if God didn't love me, He would not have blessed me so much. As for me, I have no problems with assurance whatsoever.'

• *Legalistic assurance* says that if I can only do certain good deeds in my own strength I can be assured that I am saved. This kind of assurance usually substitutes a man-made list of do's and don'ts for God's commandments in order to reduce things to a manageable level, thus promoting a form of man-centered holiness. This kind of assurance tends to begin with 'Because I...' rather than with 'Because God...'. It smacks more of the Pharisee's religion than the publican's in Jesus's parable (Luke 18:9-14).

• *Temperamental assurance* is based on innate self-confidence. Some people are very self-confident by nature and they are naturally going to have much more confidence about their state. But Scripture makes plain that assurance is more than temperament. 'Thus saith the LORD; cursed be the man that trusteth in man, and maketh flesh his arm, and whose heart departeth from the LORD' (Jer. 17:5).

• *Presumptous assurance* says, 'I am saved, and I am sure of it, so it doesn't matter how I live. I can do what I want; it doesn't matter all that much if I sin, for my sins are forgiven; I am a son of God.' Such false presumption on God's mercy produces a false assurance (cf. Rom. 6:1-18). Such people are, as Don Carson puts it, but 'nominal believers who display nothing of the promised fruits of the new covenant but who are convinced by the slogan "Once saved, always saved" that they are in no danger.'[8] Of course, if a true believer is 'once saved', he will be 'always saved', for God will not forsake the work of His own hands. But if that believer falls into a lifestyle of unrepentant sin, or takes a cavalier and indifferent attitude to sin while still claiming to be 'an assured Christian', he must be treated, as Jonathan Edwards would say, 'as an unbeliever', because either he is seriously backslidden or he is not a true believer after all. True

---

8) Don Carson, 'Reflections on Christian Assurance', *Westminster Theological Journal* 54 (1992): 28.

believers cannot indifferently persist in a lifestyle of sin (1 John 3:9), and thus cannot embrace presumptuous assurance.

• *Hyper-covenantal assurance* is a form of presumptuous assurance that bases its presumption on membership in the church as the covenant community. This form of assurance allows the covenant to dilute the need for personal faith and personal repentance. Most commonly, this assurance is strongly promoted in those Reformed and Presbyterian churches that embrace some form of 'presumptive regeneration', 'dormant regeneration', or 'covenantal regeneration' – that is, that the children of believers are deemed to have been regenerated in infancy, so believing parents are to rear them with the conviction that they are already saved, and hence do not need to tell them that they need new hearts (cf. John 3:3-8). The assurance of hyper-covenantalism tends to put all its stress on the objective gospel and minimizes the subjective gospel, so that personal communion with God plays little role in the believer's life. In this view, as William Young points out, 'Doctrinal knowledge and ethical conduct according to the Word of God are sufficient for the Christian life without any specific religious experience of conviction of sin and conversion, or any need for self-examination as to the possession of distinguishing marks of saving grace.'[9] The danger of this view is self-deceit – that is, it tends to lead children into a false profession of faith and assurance when they are still unsaved and have no genuine experiential knowledge of their own sin and depravity, faith and repentance, deliverance in Christ, communion with God, and heartfelt sanctification and gratitude.

• *Promises-only assurance* is assurance much like presumptuous assurance, only its focus is exclusively on the gospel promises of Christ as the all-in-all of assurance. Ministers who embrace this

---

9) William Young, 'Historic Calvinism and Neo-Calvinism', *Westminster Theological Journal* 36, no. 2 (1974), 166. Cf. Joel R. Beeke, *Parenting by God's Promises: How to Raise Children in the Covenant of Grace* (Orlando, Fla.: Reformation Trust, 2011), 19, and *Bringing the Gospel to Covenant Children* (Grand Rapids: Reformation Heritage Books, 2010), 4–7.

view often preach like this to their people: 'If you believe in Christ and trust in His promises only for salvation, you can be sure that you are saved. Then you don't need to examine your own soul and conscience for the marks and fruits of grace. Don't look at anything inside yourself; look only to Jesus.' That may sound good at first, but the problem is that many claim to be Christians by trusting in the gospel promises whose lives don't match their profession. This view does not square with the teaching of the apostle John in his first epistle. True, trusting in Christ alone is the primary ground of assurance, but genuine assurance also involves self-examination for marks of grace.

• *Unexamined assurance* refuses to allow itself to be inspected or examined to see whether it is real or not, contrary to 2 Corinthians 13:5. It is like a builder who, having quickly slapped together a poorly built structure, puts a Rottweiler dog on the grounds when he knows a building inspector is coming to look at it. The inspector can't get near the building. Some people are like that with their faith. They claim to have faith but they will not allow anyone – not even their pastor – to ask them how they came to that faith, or how genuine it may be.

Mike McKinley wrote most of his helpful book *Am I Really a Christian?* about the problem of false assurance, showing that you are not a Christian just because you say you are or just because you like Jesus; moreover, he continued, you are not a Christian if you are not born again, if you enjoy sin, if you don't love other people, and if you love your things more than God.

All false forms of assurance differ radically from true, biblical assurance. So how do we know if our assurance is real or not? Here are four quick tests: (1) Does it produce humility or pride? (2) Does it produce diligence and holiness, or does it make you slothful and negligent? (3) Does it make you say with the psalmist, 'Search me, O God, and know my heart: try me, and know my thoughts: and see if there be any wicked way in me, and lead me in the way everlasting' (Ps. 139:23, 24), or does it move you to say, 'Don't dare question me'? (4) Does it make you seek greater intimacy with your heavenly

Father, or does it drive you from Him so that you strive to become more independent than dependent on Him?[10]

True Assurance

Chapter 18.1 of the Confession clearly says that assurance is possible for Christians but it also stresses that assurance cannot be obtained apart from Christ. Every part of 18.1 connects assurance with Christ in saying, believe in *Him*; love *Him*; walk before *Him*. Assurance is interwoven with Christian believing, Christian loving, and fruits of faith in Christ. The essence of assurance is living in Christ.

Burgess demonstrated the possibility of assurance in a variety of ways: (1) biblical saints whose lives evidenced assurance; (2) many Scriptures that show how Christians may attain assurance (study especially John's first epistle); (3) commands in Scripture, such as 2 Peter 1:10, that Christians diligently seek assurance; (4) the right use of the sacraments which serve as assuring signs and seals for believers as God witnesses of His love to them; (5) the exercises of divine graces, such as faith, hope, love, joy, and thankfulness; (6) 'signs of grace' by which people may know they are saved, such as heartfelt sorrow for sin, demonstrating genuine meekness, hungering and thirsting after righteousness, etc. (Matt. 5:4-6); and (7) the ministry of the Holy Spirit in witnessing with our spirit by His sealing graces that we are the children of God.[11]

If assurance is not possible, Burgess concluded, then there must be some problem with its object or the means through which we obtain it. But the object of assurance is the promises of God, which are 'yea and Amen' in Christ (2 Cor. 1:20), and the means of assurance is the work of the Spirit of God, who renews the heart to sincerity and effectively works assurance. Burgess repeatedly stated the importance of the Holy Spirit's role in assurance. Without the Spirit, he said, there is no authentic assurance upon any grounds.[12]

---

10) For part of this list, I have gleaned from some notes taken from a sermon preached by David Murray.

11) *Spiritual Refining*, 2, 23–4, 676–7.

12) *Spiritual Refining*, 17, 51, 54, 59, 671.

Burgess asserted that assurance is very beneficial for our spiritual life. The nature of faith is to establish and settle us. It is a pillar and anchor to the soul. Though one can have faith without assurance, doubting and fear are the opposite of believing. Trusting in God is compared in the Bible to rolling ourselves upon Him, staying the mind on Him, and resting the heart in Him. Strong and regular exercises of faith in Christ will, over time, bring us to assurance.

How excellent is this privilege of assurance! It keeps Christians in close fellowship with God, so that they can say, 'I am my beloved's, and my beloved is mine' (Song 6:3). The Spirit of adoption puts in their hearts the attitude of a humble child, motivated to serve the Father with pure motivation (Rom. 8:14, 15). Assurance will support them when everything else in life is misery and trouble, so that they triumph over all difficulties (Rom. 8:37). Finding full rest and peace in God and Christ makes them content no matter what they lack, for He is sufficient (Ps. 73:25, 26). Therefore, how blessed is he who has God for his God, and Christ for his Christ![13]

In addition to living habitually with assurance as a seasoned believer, Thomas Brooks provided 'nine special seasons when assurance is [often] enjoyed':

- At conversion (Acts 9:33)

- Before engaging in hard or dangerous service (Matt. 17:1-6)

- During times of waiting (Ps. 40:1-3)

- During times of suffering (Acts 16:23, 24)

- During public worship, especially under sermons when God applies His Word and shines with His face upon His people (1 Thess. 1:5, 6)

- During times of personal affliction (Ps. 94:19)

- During seasons of prayer (Dan. 9:20-23)

- Before conflicts with Satan (2 Cor. 12:1-8)

---

13) *Spiritual Refining*, 59.

- After conflicts with Satan (Rev. 7:17)[14]

Though some Puritans felt that full assurance was very difficult to attain, others stressed that believers may 'ordinarily' obtain comfortable degrees of true assurance of their salvation. William Guthrie (1620–1665), a Scottish Covenanter minister who authored a classic work on assurance, *The Christian's Great Interest*, wrote: 'A man's interest in Christ, or his gracious state may be known, and that with more certainty than people conjecture; yea, and the knowledge of it may be more easily attained unto than many imagine; for not only hath the Lord commanded men to know their interest in Him as a thing attainable, but many of the saints have attained unto the clear persuasion of their interest in Christ and in God as their own God.'[15] Jonathan Edwards wrote similarly, 'A true saint may know that he has some true grace; and the more grace there is, the more easily is it known.'[16]

Lacking the Consciousness of True Assurance

Finally, chapter 18.1 of the *Westminster Confession* and the writings of Burgess emphasized a third option: believers may possess saving faith without the joy and full assurance that they possess it. Assurance augments the joy of faith, but it is not essential to salvation. Faith *alone* justifies through Christ *alone*; assurance is the conscious enjoyment of that justification and salvation.

Thus, for the Puritans, the most important question in self-examination is not, in the first place, do I possess full assurance of faith, but do I have some measure of saving faith? Do I entrust my life with all my sins into the hands of Christ? Do I trust in the promises of God? If we are saved, we must know – at least to some degree – of trusting in Christ alone. Thus, there are degrees in faith, the Puritans would say. There is weak faith, which possesses little

---

14) Brooks, *Heaven on Earth*, 53–91.

15) Guthrie, *Christian's Great Interest*, 5.

16) Jonathan Edwards, *The Religious Affections* (London: Banner of Truth Trust, 1961), 255.

assurance; there is strong faith, which possesses full assurance. Both the weak in faith and the strong in faith have the same object of faith – the Lord Jesus Christ as He is revealed in the the gospel as Savior and Lord.

A prisoner can see the sun through a small hole in the prison wall or through a prison window. A free man walking in the open air will also see the sun. There's a great difference between these two men. One is in prison; one is free. But the object of their sight is the same – the sun. And so it is with believers. Some weak believers, in their spiritual condition, often feel as if they are in prison, and yet their eyes are looking out the prison window, through the opening in the prison walls. They are gazing at the Sun of righteousness (Mal. 4:2), and though they feel bound, their heart, in hope and expectation, still goes out to Him; He is the object of their faith. Those, however, who have more assurance walk in the liberty and joy of the gospel with their heart fixed more habitually and thoroughly on Christ. Their spiritual health is much more robust and their joy more full.

Consequently, being consciously assured of possessing personal faith is necessary for spiritual health but not absolutely necessary for salvation. That's why the Puritans often said that assurance of faith belongs to the *well-being* of faith more than to the *being* of faith. That is to say, assurance belongs to the healthy condition and spiritual prosperity of faith more than to the essence of faith. Though there is some degree of assurance in every exercise of saving faith since the very nature of faith is contrary to doubt, a Christian may continue long without attaining full assurance of faith, as the child of light walking in darkness (Isa. 50:10).

Both William Perkins and Anthony Burgess are helpful in shedding further light here. Several thoughts converge in Perkins. First, Perkins taught that in weak faith God's promises are seen but the believer does not yet have freedom to appropriate them by the co-witness of the Spirit in his conscience. Second, the distinction between weak and strong faith is helpful pastorally to keep weak believers from despair by encouraging them to believe that weak faith is still authentic faith. Third, each believer must seek for strong faith, but the typical believer will not receive it 'at the first, but in some continuance of time, after that for a long space he hath kept a good conscience before God, and before men: and hath had [various] experiences of God's love and favor towards him in Christ'.[17] Finally, in strong faith, full assurance arises not as intrinsic to faith, but as a fruit of faith, ascertained by a personal, Spirit-worked appropriation of the benefits of faith.

Burgess devoted the first two sermons of *Spiritual Refining* to 'how necessary and advantageous the Assurance of our being in the state of Grace is'.[18] The advantages of assurance are so great that Burgess spoke of its necessity for four reasons: First, because of the nature of faith itself, for the more we believe in Christ alone as our Savior in a strong and habitual way, the more we will grow in assurance. Faith profits immensely from assurance. Second, 'assurance is necessary because it is part of God's glory. It is not enough that God works grace in us and sanctifies us. We must also know it, that we may praise and bless God for it.' Third, 'assurance is necessary because it gives us more joy and peace in our hearts'. Finally, 'assurance is necessary because it enlarges and quickens us to perform holy duties'.[19] Nevertheless, assurance is 'not of absolute necessity to salvation: it's not a necessary effect of our calling and election at all times'.[20]

Burgess acknowledged that many believers lack full assurance of faith. Though most believers have some degree of assurance, full assurance can be difficult for many believers to attain.[21] When a person feels the guilt of his sins, he is quick to look upon God as an enemy and an avenger. Our hearts are deceitful. We are

---

17) William Perkins, *The Works of that Famous and Worthy Minister of Christ in the Vniversitie of Cambridge, Mr. William Perkins* (London: John Legatt, 1612–1613), 1:367.

18) *Spiritual Refining*, 1–11.

19) *Faith Seeking Assurance*, 65–7 (*Spiritual Refining*, 24–5).

20) *Spiritual Refining*, 672.

21) *Spiritual Refining*, 25–6.

prone to neglect our walk with God and be spiritually careless, but assurance is preserved by a continual exercise of grace (2 Pet. 1:10). Satan attacks us with his fiery darts, and if he cannot hurt us in our obedience, he will attack us in our comforts. Pirates wait for the ships filled with gold, and Satan leaves the wicked in peace while tempting the godly with many fears. Sometimes even God hides Himself so that we will not take assurance for granted and grow lazy.

What should a person do if he has true saving grace in him, but lacks assurance? Burgess acknowledged that this is agonizing, more painful than broken bones. Let him consider whether he is living in some sin that he knows is sin, yet has not repented of it (Ps. 32:3-5; 51:8; Eph. 4:30). Let him also ask whether he is neglecting the means of grace. Assurance comes through diligent pursuit of godliness (2 Pet. 1:5-10) and prayer (Phil. 4:6, 7). If he still lacks assurance, let him remember that it is a gift of God's sovereign grace, not a natural consequence of what we do (Rom. 8:15, 16; 2 Cor. 1:3, 4). Even if you lack assurance, keep exercising love, faith, and obedience toward God.[22]

Assurance versus Presumption

Here is a summary of Burgess's teaching on how assurance and presumption must be distinguished. A false assurance is the worst delusion and insanity, but too many people bless themselves even while they are outside the door of the kingdom.[23] Assurance and presumption come from different root causes. Assurance comes from the Spirit of God enlightening the heart and working childlike affections. Presumption comes from a lack of experiential knowledge of the depth and danger of one's sin and the clinging presence of self-love and self-flattery (Prov. 16:2).

Assurance and presumption also differ in their motives and basis. Assurance comes from the Spirit of God working through

---

22) *Spiritual Refining*, 26.

23) *Faith Seeking Assurance*, 72 (*Spiritual Refining*, 27).

the Word of God to produce spiritual comfort (Rom. 15:4). Presumption comes from a natural understanding of regeneration, but regeneration cannot be spiritually understood without the Spirit's work (John 3:10). Presumption leans at least in part upon one's own merits and worthiness, but assurance looks only for sincerity of grace mingled with many faults that Christ's blood must wash away. People often presume that God loves them in a saving way because they have outward prosperity in riches, children, or honors – but they stand in slippery places and may be horribly surprised (Luke 16:25).

God generally works assurance in a manner quite different than the way presumption springs up. Though the Spirit is free to save as He pleases (John 3:8), God's ordinary way is to bring a person to sincere humiliation under the burden of his sins (Matt. 11:28). Assurance is often attained after a season of conflict with doubts and unbelief, for it is the work of the Spirit, and the flesh wars against the Spirit (Gal. 5:17). That is not to say that doubt is then fully conquered once-for-all or cannot coexist simultaneously with assurance. It is a good sign when a sense of God's grace in us comes with a feeling of our imperfections, so that we cry, 'Lord, I believe; help thou mine unbelief' (Mark 9:24).

Assurance also produces effects that go far beyond anything presumption can do. Godly assurance makes a person diligent to use the means of grace and careful to obey God's commands, but the neglect of them weakens assurance (2 Pet. 1:10). Sinful self-confidence swells all the bigger even while neglecting prayer and living in sin. Godly assurance ignites the heart with love to God, like a magnifying glass focuses the light of the sun to start a fire. Presumption works more lust for this world's goods and a proud abuse of God's gifts. Assurance has the power to support the heart when discouragements and disruptions abound and sinful confidence fails. True metal proves itself on the anvil.

We may also see the difference in the spiritual companions and enemies of assurance and presumption. Assurance comes with holy fear and trembling (Phil. 2:12), and humility and sober self-appraisal (Luke 1:46-8). Presumption shuts out godly fear, and comes with flattering self-comparison to other sinners (Luke 18:11). The only enemies of assurance are sin and coolness of zeal, for zeal is produced by God's Spirit and sin grieves the Spirit (Eph. 4:30). Presumption may be shaken by outward troubles or psychological depression, but not by sin's offense against God.[24]

God has powerful weapons to destroy the fortresses of sinful self-confidence. This is a mercy, for no one has higher obstacles against coming to Christ than the falsely assured professing Christian. God can, however, destroy these strongholds by a powerful, soul-searching preacher (2 Cor. 10:4, 5). Another weapon is an explanation and application of God's laws to the motives of the soul, as Christ did in the Sermon on the Mount (Matt. 5). God might also show people from the Bible how complete and necessary a Savior Jesus Christ is, for if He is everything, then we have nothing in ourselves. God may also accompany the thunder of the Word with the afflictions of earthly grief to awaken sinners. He can use the frightening examples of people who seemed so spiritual (and thought so highly of themselves) but then fell horribly. Indeed, God can use foolish decisions people make in other areas of life to show them that they may be fooling themselves about their spiritual state too.[25]

Concluding Questions for Self-examination

Are you a true believer who consciously enjoys true assurance? Or, do you believe that salvation is in Christ alone, but you lack the conscious assurance that that salvation is also for you personally? Or, are you perhaps someone who claims to be a Christian but your salvation is not grounded in Christ alone, such that you only possess false assurance of faith?

If you lack assurance of faith but cannot deny that Christ is your only hope for salvation, I hope you are asking at this point: How may I gain assurance and know that I possess it? If you do have some

---

24) *Faith Seeking Assurance*, 72–87 (*Spiritual Refining*, 27–32).

25) *Faith Seeking Assurance*, 89–93 (*Spiritual Refining*, 33–4).

degree of assurance of faith, I hope you are asking at this point: How may I grow in this assurance? If you fear that you have only false assurance, I hope you are asking at this point: How may I find true assurance; or, in some cases, how may I be saved? I trust that the next chapter will answer these questions for you in a clear manner.

❦ 5 ❦

Assurance from God's Promises

If the evidence of God's saving work in the believer's life appears to him as 'muddied waters, the proper duty of a godly man is to throw himself boldly upon the promises [of God],...to go unto God, and rely upon him, in which sense Job said, Though he kill me, yet will I trust in him (Job 13:15)'. So said Anthony Burgess, one of the Westminster Assembly's most insightful writers on assurance of faith.

Thomas Brooks put it this way in the concluding sentence of his magisterial *Cabinet of Jewels*: 'Now, when any fears, or darkness, or doubts, or disputes arise in your souls about your spiritual state, oh, then, run to Christ in the promise, and plead the promise, and... let your souls cleave close to the promise: for this is the way of ways to have your evidences cleared, your comforts restored, your peace maintained, your graces strengthened, and your assurance raised and confirmed.'[1]

In the last chapter we looked at the first paragraph of the Westminster Confession, chapter 18, that unveiled three possibilities regarding assurance: having false assurance, having true assurance,

---

1) Thomas Brooks, 'A Cabinet of Jewels', in *The Works of Thomas Brooks*, ed. A. Grosart (1864; reprint, Edinburgh: Banner of Truth Trust, 1980), 3:504.

and having saving faith but lacking assurance that we possess it. Now we turn to the second paragraph of chapter 18, which is the heart of how to realize assurance of faith:

> This certainty is not a bare conjectural and probable persuasion grounded upon a fallible hope; but an infallible assurance of faith founded upon the divine truth of the promises of salvation, the inward evidence of those graces unto which these promises are made, the testimony of the Spirit of adoption witnessing with our spirits that we are the children of God, which Spirit is the earnest of our inheritance, whereby we are sealed to the day of redemption.

The Foundations of Assurance

The Westminster Confession identifies the foundations of assurance in chapter 18.2. It is important here not to confuse the foundations or grounds of *assurance* with the foundations or grounds of *salvation*.[2] As John Murray said, 'When we speak of the grounds of assurance, we are thinking of the ways in which a believer comes to entertain this assurance, not of the grounds on which his salvation rests. The grounds of salvation are as secure for the person who does not have full assurance as for the person who has.'[3]

In this sense, 18.2 presents a complex ground of assurance,[4] which includes a primary, objective ground ('the divine truth of the promises of salvation') and two secondary, subjective grounds ('the inward evidence of those graces unto which these promises are made' and 'the testimony of the Spirit of adoption witnessing with our spirits'). Let's look at all three of these in separate chapters, beginning here with the objective ground of assurance.

---

2) Paul Helm, *Calvin and the Calvinists* (Edinburgh: Banner of Truth Trust, 1982), 28, 75.

3) John Murray, *Collected Writings* (Edinburgh: Banner of Truth Trust, 1980), 2:270.

4) James Buchanan, *The Doctrine of Justification: An Outline of Its History in the Church and of Its Exposition from Scripture* (Edinburgh: T. & T. Clark, 1867), 184. Cf. Louis Berkhof, *The Assurance of Faith* (Grand Rapids: Eerdmans, 1939), 49–68.

Divine Promises in Christ

The Puritans believed that God's promises in Christ are the primary ground for a believer's assurance. Thomas Brooks wrote, 'The promises of God are a Christian's *magna charta*, his chiefest evidences for heaven. Divine promises are God's deed of gift; they are the only assurance which the saints must show for their right and title to Christ, to His blood, and to all the happiness and blessedness that comes by Him.... The promises are not only the food of faith, but also the very life and soul of faith; they are a mine of rich treasures, a garden full of the choicest and sweetest flowers; in them are wrapped up all celestial contentments and delights.'[5] Burgess said that it 'is a more noble and excellent way' to find assurance of faith by relying upon God's promise in Christ outside of us than it is to come to assurance by being assured of the evidences of grace within us.[6] That emphasis on God's promises in Christ implies several things for our experience of assurance.

First, we do not gain assurance by looking at ourselves or anything we have produced apart from God's promises, but first of all by looking to God's faithfulness in Christ as He is revealed in the promises of the gospel. The same offers of grace and gospel promises that lead us to salvation are sufficient to lead us to assurance.

Paul tells us in 2 Corinthians 1:18-20 that God's gospel promises in Christ cannot fail because God's character is true and faithful: 'But as God is true, our word toward you was not yea and nay. For the Son of God, Jesus Christ, who was preached among you...was not yea and nay, but in him was yea. For all the promises of God in him are yea, and in him Amen, unto the glory of God by us.' God doesn't speak out of both sides of His mouth, Paul says. God's Word is always trustworthy.

Jesus Christ is God's everlasting 'yea' and 'amen'. While they were together in eternity, and then when Christ took our frail flesh and lived among us, and now in heaven at God's right hand, Christ

---

5) Brooks, 'A Cabinet of Jewels', in *Works*, 3:254–5.

6) *Faith Seeking Assurance*, 140 (*Spiritual Refining*, 51).

has always been God's great 'yes!' God has had no second plan, no second thoughts. He has no need to send another Jesus, or more apostles. All of salvation and life for all eternity is in His glorious Son, and in Him alone. Christ is the affirmation of God's love for sinners. When He says, 'Come to me and trust my promises in my Son', Jesus is God's 'yes', so God means that you, personally and particularly, are to come to Him just as you are and not wait until you are better. Paul says we don't preach both 'yes' and 'no': 'yes' you may come, but 'no' you may not come just yet, since you must make yourself better first. Rather, we preach 'yes', you may and must come to the Son of God, Jesus Christ, now: 'Believe on the Lord Jesus Christ, and thou shalt be saved' (Acts 16:31).

Thus, our assurance lies in the character of our faithful God, who manifests Himself in the unchangeable person and finished work of His Son. Read the Gospels about Him, and learn that the God and Father of Jesus Christ is not an insincere deity. He tells you that you are in trouble because of your sin, but He also tells you that He is more than willing to rescue sinners just like you through Christ when you come to Him.

In His death, Christ didn't just make salvation possible for us. His death truly saves those who believe in Him (Col. 1:13, 14). Assurance thrives on the knowledge that Christ accomplished redemption for us on the cross. Assurance thrives when we realize that God did not rescue Christ from the cross because He was rescuing us through Christ's perfectly obedient life and His sin-atoning death. While God was bringing darkness over Jerusalem during the crucifixion, dear believer, He was bringing us into His kingdom of light. As Jesus bled, God the Son was paying the price for our redemption from sin's guilt. If you have been brought to repentance and to trust in and to love God's Son, assurance can thrive for you because of what God did for your sake through the 'yes' work of His Son. Don't doubt, but enjoy the assurance that God has settled your account forever because He is satisfied with the Christ for every one of His repenting, believing people. Since Jesus Christ is sufficient to be God's 'yea and Amen', you ought to regard

His saving work of substitutionary obedience entirely sufficient for your salvation.

Believers in Christ are assured of salvation in the very first place because their God and their salvation are true, sure, perfect, and unchangeable in Jesus Christ forever. Our salvation and security in Christ, therefore, rest on:

- the unchangeability of God Himself: 'I am the LORD, I change not; therefore ye sons of Jacob are not consumed' (Mal. 3:6);

- the eternality of God's electing love: 'I have loved thee with an everlasting love: therefore with lovingkindness have I drawn thee' (Jer. 31:3);

- the irrevocability of God's gifts: 'For the gifts and calling of God are without repentance' (Rom. 11:29; cf. 1 Cor. 2:12);

- the inviolability of God's oath (Heb. 6:17-20);

- the perfection of Christ's work as Mediator (Heb. 10:19-23); and

- the sovereignty of the Spirit's application of that work (1 Cor. 2:10-14).[7]

When Paul expresses his assurance of salvation in 2 Timothy 1:12, notice how firmly he grounds that assurance in the trustworthiness of God in His Son: 'I know whom I have believed, and am persuaded that he is able to keep that which I have committed unto him against that day.' Paul does not rely on his reputation or on what he had done, but on God's trustworthiness. His assurance rests on the character of God; God is unchangeably good to sinners in Christ Jesus. As James says, 'Every good gift and every perfect gift is from above, and cometh down from the Father of lights, with whom is no variableness, neither shadow of turning' (1:17).

---

7) For a fuller treatment of most of these points, see Michael Barrett, *Complete in Him* (Grand Rapids: Reformation Heritage Books, 2017), 252–62.

The gods of Greece and Rome were thought to be powerful, but neither loving nor good – and dangerous because they were so capricious and changeable. Our God is not like that, says Paul. He is utterly true and trustworthy. For Christ's sake, He is merciful and will not cast out any who come to Him (John 6:37). He delights in mercy – that's who He is – that's His character (Micah 7:18). You and I can have assurance that the almighty yet tenderly merciful Father will not reject us when we believe in His Son and ask Him for His Spirit. Jesus says, 'If ye, then, being evil, know how to give good gifts unto your children: how much more shall your heavenly Father give the Holy Spirit to them that ask him?' (Luke 11:13).

Because of the true, merciful, and unchangeable character of God, we can be sure that our relationship with Him, in Christ, is everlasting, and not temporary. Philippians 1:6 says, 'Being confident of this very thing, that he which hath begun a good work in you will perform it until the day of Jesus Christ.' Paul is saying that God did not begin the 'good work' of making you like Christ only to abandon that work now or at some point in the future because He is no longer able or willing to complete it. No, God's gospel, God's promises, and our salvation are all 'yes', not 'yes and no', because God and His gospel are trustworthy.

When expounding the Luke 7 account of the woman who was forgiven and received assurance, Burgess wrote, '*As soon as she repented in her heart of her evil ways, and believed in Christ, her sins were forgiven her;* for so God doth promise; and this was before she came to Christ, but she cometh to Christ for the more assurance of pardon…. How could she come to know her sins were forgiven before Christ told her? I answer, By the promise of God made to every true penitent and believer: though this assurance of hers was imperfect, and therefore admitted of further degrees' (emphasis added).[8]

---

8) Anthony Burgess, *The True Doctrine of Iustification Asserted and Vindicated, From the Errors of Papists, Arminians, Socinians, and more especially Antinomians* (London: Robert White for Thomas Vnderhil, 1648), 269–70.

Second, as assurance grows, God's promises become increasingly real to the believer personally and experientially. The promises of God and assurance of faith reinforce each other. Jonathan Edwards believed that assurance is first of all based upon an awareness of having spiritually applied the promises of God to the heart:

> A spiritual application of the Word of God consists in applying it to the heart, in spiritually enlightening, sanctifying influences. A spiritual application of an invitation or offer of the gospel consists in giving the soul a spiritual sense or relish of the holy and divine blessings offered, and also the sweet and wonderful grace of the offerer, in making so gracious an offer, and of his holy excellency and faithfulness to fulfill what he offers, and his glorious sufficiency for it; so leading and drawing forth the heart to embrace the offer; and thus giving the man evidence of his title to the thing offered.[9]

When we have an experiential knowledge of God's promises, then our hearts echo the truth of God's promises. As we read the promises of God to us, we confess that all our salvation is based on them, and we find their truth verified in our soul. When we compare the promises of God in Scripture with what we have experienced, we must conclude, 'My salvation is proven! God's promises shall never fail me.'[10]

God's promises are the pathways on which Christ meets the soul. So Thomas Goodwin wrote, 'If one promise belongs to thee, then all do; for every one conveys [the] whole Christ in whom all the promises are made and who is the matter of them.'[11] Another Puritan, William Spurstowe (c. 1605–1666), wrote, 'The promises are instrumental in the coming of Christ and the soul together; they are the warrant by which faith is emboldened to come to him, and take hold of him; but the union which faith makes is

---

9) *The Works of Jonathan Edwards* (hereafter: *WJE*) (New Haven, Conn.: Yale University Press, 1959), 2:225.

10) *Faith Seeking Assurance*, 14 (*Spiritual Refining*, 5–6).

11) Goodwin, *Works*, 3:321.

not between a believer and the promise, but between a believer and Christ.'[12]

Spurstowe went on to use two beautiful word pictures to show what it means to appropriate the gospel promises of God experientially. First, God takes the thousands of gospel promises in His Word and puts them all like golden coins in a large bag and then pours them out at the feet of needy, confessing, believing sinners, and says, 'Take whatever you will!' Second, God's gospel promises are like stars at night, Spurstowe said. When you first walk outside in the country late at night you look up into the sky and see a few stars, but the longer you gaze up at the sky and your eyes get increasingly used to the night light, the more stars you see, until 'the whole firmament, from every quarter, with a numberless multitude of stars, is richly enammelled as with so many golden studs'.[13] So when Christians begin to meditate on God's promises, the number of promises and the light coming from them may at first seem to be small and weak, so as to be insufficient to quell our fears and dispel our darkness, but when we read and meditate further, and begin to see the thousands of promises in the Scripture together with the bright light that shines from them clearly and distinctly, our souls are then ravished and filled with delight and assurance.[14] Then it is as if Christ and we meet together with assured joy in the promises that speak assurance to our souls of Him.

Third, the Christ-centeredness of personal assurance is accented in God's promises, for Jesus Christ Himself is the 'sum, fountain, seal, treasury of all the promises' of God.[15] Reynolds explained: 'All

---

12) William Spurstowe, *The Wells of Salvation Opened: or, A Treatise discerning the nature, preciousness, and usefulness of the Gospel Promises and Rules for the Right Application of Them* (London: T. R. & E. M. for Ralph Smith, 1655), 44–5.

13) Spurstowe, *The Wells of Salvation Opened*, 78–9.

14) Spurstowe, *The Wells of Salvation Opened*, 79.

15) Edward Reynolds, *Three Treatises of the Vanity of the Creature. The Sinfulnesse of Sinne. The Life of Christ* (London: B. B. for Rob Bastocke and George Badger, 1642), 1:365.

the promises are made in Christ being purchased by his merits, and they are all performed in Christ, being administered by his power and office.... Promises...are the rays and beams of Christ the Sun of Righteousness, in whom they are all founded and established.... Every promise apprehended by faith carries a man to Christ, and to the consideration of our unity with him, in the right whereof we have claim to the promises.'[16] 'Let thy eye and heart, first, most, and last, be fixed upon Christ, then will assurance bed and board with thee,' said Brooks.[17]

In this regard, Burgess wrote:

> We should not so gaze upon ourselves to find graces in our hearts that we forget those acts of faith whereby we immediately close with Christ and rely upon Him only for our justification. The fear of doing this has made some deny the validity of using signs as evidence of our justification. And indeed it is true that many of God's children, while they are studying and examining themselves to see whether grace is in their souls (and that upon the discovery of graces, are persuaded of their justification), may very much neglect those choice and principal acts of faith whereby they may have an acquiescency and recumbency upon Christ for acceptation with God. This is as if old Jacob rejoiced so much about the chariot Joseph sent, whereby he knew that his son was alive, that he failed to desire to see Joseph himself. Thus while you are so full of joy about perceiving grace in your soul, you forget to joy in Christ Himself, who is more excellent than all your graces.[18]

Perhaps Rutherford summarized this point best when he stated in his catechism, 'The new covenant is a mass of promises laying the weight of our salvation upon a stronger one than we are, to wit, upon Christ, and faith grips [i.e., grasps or seizes hold of] the promises and makes us go out of ourselves to Christ as being at home [i.e, familiar] with Christ.'[19]

---

16) Reynolds, *Three Treatises*, 1:345, 356–7.

17) Brooks, *Heaven on Earth*, 307.

18) *Faith Seeking Assurance*, 114–15 (*Spiritual Refining*, 41).

19) *Catechisms of the Second Reformation*, ed. Alex Mitchell, 176.

Finally, though subjective phenomena may sometimes *feel* more real than faith in God's promises, such experiences give less glory to God than divine promises apprehended directly by faith. Burgess said, 'Trusting in God and in Christ when we feel nothing but guilt and destruction in ourselves is the greatest honor we can give to God. Therefore, though living by signs is more comfortable to us, living by faith is a greater honor to God.'[20] Brooks said it even more strongly:

> Though the sight of a Christian's graces and gracious evidences be very comfortable and delightful to him, yet the sight of Christ should be ten thousand times more comfortable and delightful to him.... What are the friends of the bridegroom to the bridegroom himself?... No more are all a Christian's graces or gracious evidence to the Lord Jesus himself. A Christian should say to all his gifts, graces, evidences, and services, Stand by, make room for Christ, make room for Christ. Oh, none but Christ! Oh, none [compared] to Christ! Living by signs is most natural, pleasing and comfortable to us, but living by faith is most honorable to Christ. It is said, 'the just shall live by his faith,' not by his evidences (Hab. 2:4; Heb. 10:38).[21]

No Puritan has been accused of being overly introspective as much as Thomas Hooker (1586–1647), a prominent colonial leader often called 'the Father of Connecticut'. Some have argued that he was more concerned about the response of a believer's senses to the 'sweetness' of the Spirit than he was about faith. Norman Pettit writes, 'Hooker, more than any other preacher in his day, described the order of salvation as a process thoroughly mixed with hopes and fears. Man should expect, as he does in life, to confront both joy and doubt.'[22] Yet even Hooker said that God's covenant promises of eternal life are 'far more important than sensation and taste'. Hooker wrote, 'A man's faith may be somewhat strong when his feeling is

---

20) *Faith Seeking Assurance*, 156 (*Spiritual Refining*, 57).

21) Brooks, 'A Cabinet of Choice Jewels', in *Works*, 3:502.

22) Norman Pettit, 'Hooker's Doctrine of Assurance: A Critical Phase in New England Spiritual Thought', *New England Quarterly* 47 (1974):534.

nothing at all. Therefore away with your sense and feeling, and go to the promise.'[23]

Moreover, the smallest degree of saving faith in God's promises will prove as effectual as full assurance of faith in God's promises. Though a spider's thread connected to a rock is much weaker than a strong anchor connected to that rock, the rock is equally strong. So a weak faith that casts itself on Christ and His promises shall find that the Lord Jesus Christ is just as much the rock of salvation for that trembling soul as He is for one who has full assurance of faith. As Brooks wrote,

> *The least degree of grace, if true, is sufficient to salvation;* for the promises of life and glory, of remission and salvation, of everlasting happiness and blessedness, are not made [in relation] to degrees of grace, but to the truth of grace; not to faith in triumph, but to faith in truth; and therefore the sense and evidence of the least grace, yea, of the least degree of the least grace, may afford some measure of assurance.[24]

Concluding Applications

When Christian was confined in Doubting Castle in *Pilgrim's Progress*, Giant Despair beat him and threatened to kill him the next day. But that night Christian remembered he had 'the key of promise' in his pocket. Using that key, he quickly opened all the castle's locks and escaped. Bunyan's message is unmistakable: we don't need a personal revelation or experience to believe that those promises are given to us.

When we fear that since our heart is desperately wicked we may therefore be deceiving ourselves when we think we are trusting God's promises, we must remember that in His Word, God pours His promises in Jesus Christ at our feet, and grants poor sinners like us to freely use them. We need not fear, since God loves to see His children scoop up His promises and put them to good use.

---

23) Thomas Hooker, *The Soul's Implantation* (London, 1637), 233, cited in Pettit, 'Hooker's Doctrine of Assurance', 521.

24) Brooks, *Works*, 3:259.

We need not be shy to simply embrace and believe them, that is, to believe in Jesus Christ who is the content of these promises. As we do so, we discover to our astonishment and joy that Giant Despair is powerless to keep us as his prisoner. The gospel promises of God in Christ are mightier than all the arsenals of Satan and his minions. As Michael Barrett quips, 'Assurance of salvation does not result from the power of positive thinking; it flows from the power of the gospel of Jesus Christ.'[25]

But you may ask, how do I know I am truly living out of God's promises in Christ, and therefore have a saving interest in them and may draw assurance of faith from them? Thomas Brooks offered nine ways 'a person may know whether he has a real and saving interest in the promises or no'.[26] Many of these tests deal with subjective fruits in the believer that flow out of properly embracing God's objective promises in Christ. They include:

- resting my soul upon God's promises, appropriating those promises to myself;

- subjecting myself gratefully to God's words of command, revealing that His words of promise most assuredly belong to me;

- waiting on God for the fulfilling of His promises, notwithstanding many objections, discouragements, and difficulties;

- having within me those divine graces to which these promises are made, such as faith, repentance, love, fear, hope, and patience;

- living on God's promises as my daily food;

- being united and married to Christ by faith;

- embracing even one of God's promises allows me to boldly conclude my saving interest in every divine promise;

---

25) Barrett, *Complete in Him*, 264.
26) Brooks, *Works*, 3:254–9.

- flying to God's precious promises in my great trials; and

- valuing God's promises more than anything in this world.

Burgess agreed. The promises of God don't exist in a vacuum, he said. They are applied to the soul unto assurance, and that application produces *'an holy and humble walking'*. For proof, Burgess quoted 2 Corinthians 7:1, 'Having therefore these promises, dearly beloved, let us cleanse ourselves from all filthiness of the flesh and spirit, perfecting holiness in the fear of God.' Burgess concluded, 'The more gracious then we perceive God to us, the more humiliation and debasement we find in ourselves.'[27]

Burgess and his colleagues consistently reminded us that the objective promise embraced by faith is infallible because it is *God's* comprehensive and faithful covenant promise. Consequently, subjective evidence, though necessary, must always be regarded as secondary, for it is often mixed with human convictions and feelings even when it gazes upon the work of God. All exercises of saving faith apprehend to some degree the primary ground of divine promises in Christ.

---

27) Burgess, *The True Doctrine of Iustification*, 272.

❧ 6 ❧

Assurance from Evidences of Grace

Some Christians, including many preachers, think today that the last chapter's subject – assurance from the promises of God – is the be-all and end-all of the doctrine of assurance. They reason that if God's promises in Christ are the primary foundation of assurance, nothing else is needed. Since our human nature is deceitful, it is best, they think, to never look for signs or fruits of grace within oneself. Objective assurance outside of ourselves is all that we need. Self-examination will either puff us up with false pride or bring us to despair when we realize how much sin still lives within us.

There is an element of truth in what they are saying. If we examine ourselves only by ourselves – apart from the Bible, from Jesus, and from the Holy Spirit – we will indeed always be prone to err. John Calvin even said that such self-examination will only lead us to sure damnation.[1]

But Calvin also said something else. He realized that there were many 'Christians' in his own day who claimed assurance of grace and salvation because they trusted in the promises of God alone for salvation, but whose lives did not bear the fruit of their profession.

---

1) For an explanation of Calvin's views on self-examination, see my *Quest for Full Assurance of Faith*, 59–64.

How much more true that is today – and especially in America, where most of the population claim to be Christians but only a minority reflect genuine saving faith in their lives. Jesus put it this way, 'Ye shall know them by their fruits' (Matt. 7:16). And the apostle John repeatedly identified the fruits that we need to possess if we would have assurance that we are true believers (1 John 2:3, 5; 3:14; 5:2).

The proof of conversion is the fruit that it bears, not the number, character or duration of our experiences, or the stages by which they unfold. Though God ordinarily saves sinners first by awakening them to their sin and His wrath, then bringing them to faith and peace in Christ, a set pattern of experiences is not essential to conversion, whereas a new nature demonstrated in bearing practical fruit is. As Edwards wrote: 'That which distinguishes the profitable hearers of God's Word from all others, is that they understand it and bring forth the fruit of it.'[2]

So how must self-examination be done today? What are the fruits we are to look for? How are we to engage in that search? How can we be sure that our search is accurate? These are the kinds of questions that thoughtful Christians have asked in the past and are still asking today.

The *Westminster Confession* addresses such questions as these when it says in the last half of 18.2 that assurance of faith is grounded not only on the promises of God embraced by faith, but also on

> …the inward evidence of those graces unto which these promises are made, the testimony of the Spirit of adoption witnessing with our spirits that we are the children of God, which Spirit is the earnest of our inheritance, whereby we are sealed to the day of redemption.

The Logic of Assurance

The Puritans coveted a life that showed Christ's presence in the believer. They were convinced that the grace of God within believers confirms the reality of faith. William Ames wrote, 'He that rightly

---

2) *WJE*, 16:748; 14:243–5.

understands the promise of the covenant, cannot be sure of his salvation, unless he perceives in himself true faith and repentance.'[3] They searched for the grace of God at work in believers by means of logical arguments called 'syllogisms', based on the so-called reflex or reflective act of faith.[4] The language of syllogism and reflex acts of faith may sound difficult to understand, but it is really not as we use these methods almost instinctively to examine ourselves nearly every day. What it amounts to is simply this: By the reflective act of faith, the Holy Spirit sheds light upon His work in the believer, enabling him to conclude that his faith is saving because its exercises have a saving character. Thus, the logic of assurance involves the act of faith looking at itself or viewing its reflection in its acts in response to God and His Word. Burgess put it this way:

> First, there are the *direct acts* of the soul, whereby the soul immediately and directly responds to some object. Second, there are *reflex acts* of the soul, by which the soul considers and observes what acts it does. It's as if the eye is turned inward to see itself. The Apostle John expresses this fully, saying, 'We do know that we know' (1 John 2:3). So, when we believe in God, that is a direct act of the soul; when we repent of sin, because God is dishonored, that is a direct act; but when we know that we do believe, and that we do repent of our sin, that is a reflex act.[5]

Burgess and the Puritans talked about two closely related, yet distinct, syllogisms that fortify assurance – the practical (outward) syllogism and the mystical (inward) syllogism.[6] The practical syllogism was based on the believer's sanctification and good works in daily life. It emphasized the believer's life of obedience that

---

3) William Ames, *The Marrow of Theology*, trans. John D. Eusden (Boston: Pilgrim Press, 1968), 1.3.22.

4) John Flavel, *The Works of John Flavel* (reprint ed., London: Banner of Truth Trust, 1968), 2:330.

5) *Spiritual Refining*, 672.

6) Cornelis Graafland, 'Van *syllogismus practicus* naar *syllogismus mysticus*', in *Wegen en Gestalten in het Gereformeerd Protestantisme*, ed. W. Balke, C. Graafland, and H. Harkema (Amsterdam: Ton Bolland, 1976), 105–22.

confirmed his experience of grace. It went something like this. *Major premise*: According to Scripture, only those who possess saving faith will receive the Spirit's testimony that their lives manifest fruits of sanctification and good works. *Minor premise*: I cannot deny that by the grace of God I have received the Spirit's testimony that I manifest fruits of sanctification and good works. *Conclusion*: I am a partaker of saving faith.

The practical syllogism was based on texts which teach that orthodoxy produces orthopraxy – that is, that right believing must produce right living.[7] Paul usually follows this twofold order in his epistles (e.g., orthodoxy in Ephesians 1–3 and orthopraxy in Ephesians 4–6), and the Puritans followed suit in their sermons, first preaching doctrine and then practice ('uses'). They held that sermons had to be heard in faith and acted on or lived out in faith. Sanctification must follow justification because both flow out of union with Christ. The promises of God embraced compel the living out of those promises in a daily Christian lifestyle. Sanctification and good works visualize election. Consequently, the Puritans emphasized that texts such as 2 Peter 1:5-10 (stressing virtue, knowledge, temperance, patience, godliness, and brotherly love as fruits of faith),[8] and other statements in 1 John stressing the Christian walk, were great helps to assurance by means of the practical syllogism. The First Epistle of John often uses the practical syllogism in a succinct form. For example: 'Hereby we do know that we know him, if we keep his commandments' (2:3); that is, those who know Him keep His commandments; I keep His commandments; therefore I know that I know Him (cf. 3:14; 5:2).

William Perkins provided additional marks or signs of grace from First John by which the believer may examine himself syllogistically.

---

7) Ryan Glomsrud, 'The Problem of Assurance', *Modern Reformation* 21, no. 2 (2012):58–9.

8) Cornelius Burgess, *A Chain of Graces drawn out at length for a Reformation of Manners. Or, A brief Treatise of Virtue, Knowledge, Temperance, Patience, Godliness, Brotherly kindness, and Charity, so far as they are urged by the Apostle, in 2 Pet. 1. 5, 6, 7* (London, 1622), 32.

In each case, the major premise is something true of believers in general; if it be true of you, then you should be assured that you are a Christian. Here is Perkins's list:

1. Sincerity of life and religion is a mark of communion with God (1:7).

2. Humble confession of sin to God is a mark of remission of sin (1:9).

3. Delighting in God and His grace is a mark of saving faith (2:13).

4. Fleeing the world's lusts is a sign of love for Christ (2:16).

5. God's Spirit dwelling in the heart is a sign of perseverance (2:20).

6. Perseverance in the knowledge and obedience of the gospel is a sign of communion with Christ (2:25).

7. Purifying oneself is a sign of adoption (3:3).

8. To love a Christian because he is a godly person is a mark of being God's child (3:14).

9. Compassion stirring in the heart is a mark of love (3:17).

10. Works of mercy are marks of love (3:18).

11. Boldness in prayer is a sign of a pacified conscience (3:20).

12. The operation of God's Spirit in sanctifying us is a sign of communion with God (3:24).

13. To be like God in holiness of life is a sign of his love to us particularly (4:17).

14. Our love to God is a sign that he loves us (4:19).[9]

The mystical syllogism was based largely on the believer's internal exercises and progress in sanctification. It focused more on the

---

9) Perkins, *Works*, 1:423–8.

inward man and went something like this. *Major premise*: According to Scripture, only those who possess saving faith will so experience the Spirit's confirmation of inward grace and godliness that self will decrease and Christ will increase. *Minor premise*: I cannot deny that by the grace of God I experience the Spirit's testimony confirming inward grace and godliness such that I decrease and Christ increases. *Conclusion*: I am a partaker of saving faith.

The mystical syllogism employs a variety of evidences. Burgess wrote, 'Sometimes the fear of God is a sign, sometimes a poverty of spirit, sometimes hungering and thirsting after righteousness, sometimes repentance, sometimes love, and sometimes patience. If a godly man can find any of these signs in himself he may be assured of his salvation and justification, even though he does not see all the signs in himself.'[10]

By the 1640s, Puritans were accepting the mystical syllogism on a par with the practical syllogism.[11] Consequently, some Puritans, including Burgess, were fond of answering the great case of conscience, 'How do I know whether or not I am a believer?' by offering a combination of signs that included the good works of the practical syllogism as well as the inner sanctifying marks of the mystical syllogism. For example, after preaching eleven sermons on assurance, Burgess delivered eight messages on the true signs of grace and fifteen more on the false signs of grace. True signs include obedience, sincerity, grief over indwelling sin as well as opposition to and abstinence from sin, openness to divine examination, growth in grace, spiritual performance of duties, and love to the godly. Signs that could fall short of saving grace include outward church privileges; spiritual gifts; affections of the heart in holy things; judgments and opinions about spiritual truth; great sufferings for Christ; strictness in religion; zeal in false worship; external obedience to the law of God; a belief of the truths of religion; a peaceable frame of heart and persuasion of God's love; outward success; prosperity and greatness

---

10) *Faith Seeking Assurance*, 115 (*Spiritual Refining*, 41).

11) Graafland, 'Van *syllogismus practicus* naar *syllogismus mysticus*,' 105.

in the world; and an abandonment of gross sins. The section on false signs concludes with a sermon on 'the difficulty, and in some sense, impossibility of salvation, notwithstanding' how easy people may imagine it to be.

In a sermon on 'The Lawfulness and Obligation of Proceeding by Signs' – that is, using inward evidences of grace to increase a personal sense of assurance – Burgess answered six objections against the use of syllogisms and the reflex act of faith. In the fifth objection he came to the heart of the matter:

> *Objection 5: It is difficult, if not impossible, to have certainty by means of signs. For any sign, such as love of the brethren, must first be explained as the love that exists because people are brothers and have the kind of love that proceeds from upright principles, pure motives, and many other qualifications, which are as hard to know as the inward root of grace itself.*

Answer 1. First, Scripture gives many signs and symptoms of grace, so if a man cannot find all of them in himself, yet discovers some – even only one – he may conclude that all the rest are there. This is because the harmony and connection of grace is compared to the image of God, which consists of all its due lineaments. Thus it is wrong for a Christian who can find little of God's Spirit in him to doubt that he has nothing at all.

Answer 2. There is a twofold knowledge. One is distinct and demonstrative; it is *a priori*, from the cause to the effect. With this we know the principles and root of grace within us and may thus proceed to the effects of it. The other is more general and proceeds from effects to the cause, or *a posteriori*. With this we proceed from the streams to the fountain. This kind of knowledge is the easiest to grasp. We are also most prone to think in terms of effects to cause. The Spirit of God generally guides us in this way since it is most suitable to our natures.

Answer 3. Though a man may doubt some signs, it does not follow that he will doubt all of them because he may be tempted to favor one sign more than another and perceive one sign more easily than another. So a godly man may argue from what is less known to what is more known.[12]

---

12) *Faith Seeking Assurance*, 146–8 (*Spiritual Refining*, 52–3).

Burgess used the syllogism of the Spirit's work to help believers toward assurance by directing them, in the tradition of other Reformers like Theodore Beza and William Perkins, to grasp any link of the order of salvation to 'press toward the mark for the prize of the high calling of God in Christ Jesus' (Phil. 3:14). Burgess said, '[Since] it is more difficult to find some [signs of grace] in our selves than others, yet we may proceed from those that are easier to see to those that are more difficult.'[13]

Free-Will Overtones?

Burgess was aware of possible 'free-will' overtones in the reflex act of faith and took pains to keep it within the confines of the doctrines of grace by further analysis of the syllogism.

First, Burgess stated that assurance obtained by using a syllogism was itself the work of the Spirit of God. All believers were forbidden to trust in their *own* trusting or the conclusions they drew from it, apart from the Spirit. Burgess insisted we must not separate the Spirit's work from the syllogistic, reflex act of faith:

> We do not say that the graces of God's Spirit can or do witness by themselves, for the sealing and witnessing are efficiently from the Spirit of God and are only the means by which God's Spirit makes Himself known. As colors cannot be seen on an object without light shining upon them, so neither can we behold the good things God has wrought for us without the aid of the Spirit of God…. In philosophy, reason makes the major and minor in any syllogism. In spiritual things, the Spirit of God enables a man to make a whole syllogism for a believer's comfort and establishment.[14]

Burgess concluded that if we desire to increase our assurance by employing the syllogism we must 'above all, pray to God for His Spirit, so as to enlighten our eyes…. For the Spirit of God is the efficient cause of all this certainty.'[15]

---

13) *Faith Seeking Assurance*, 148 (*Spiritual Refining*, 53).

14) *Faith Seeking Assurance*, 142, 149 (*Spiritual Refining*, 51, 54).

15) *Faith Seeking Assurance*, 162 (*Spiritual Refining*, 59).

Let me explain as simply as I can how the Holy Spirit does this work. The Holy Spirit works in our soul the marks of grace: He changes our nature, makes us a new creation, renews us from within, works real faith and real repentance in us, and puts us on the pathway of obedience so that we hunger and thirst after Christ's righteousness, and we long to mind the things of the Spirit and obey all the Ten Commandments perfectly from the heart. He does all these things in us and then He shows us that He does those things in us. Our conscience then testifies that even though we don't have any of these marks of grace to the degree we wish we had them, we can't deny that we do have at least something of some of them experientially and they are precious to us. And we know we couldn't have anything of any of them without the Holy Spirit.

For example, every believer knows deep down that he would never hunger and thirst after Christ's righteousness (Matt. 5:6) without the Holy Spirit working that hunger and thirst in him. Even as the Holy Spirit is testifying in me that this is true, my conscience is also co-witnessing with me that I cannot deny that I do hunger and thirst after Christ's righteousness. By the Spirit's grace, I know that I know that I yearn for Him and His righteousness and His salvation.

Second, Burgess said the syllogism flowed out of the living Word, Jesus Christ, and was based on the written Word for its very framework. The reflex act of faith arises from the believer seeing in himself Christ's distinguishing graces as they conform to the Word of God. Burgess wrote: 'When the apostle John commands us to examine and prove ourselves, he supposes there is a sure canon and rule by which we may measure and regulate those things we doubt, and this is the Word of God.... Scriptural godliness is as different from a moral man's godliness as the sun is from a glow worm.'[16]

Third, Burgess said the syllogism and reflex act only have a secondary status. He wrote:

> Though the perception of our graces may be of some comfort, Christ Himself ought to be much more comfort to us, for graces are only the

---

16) *Faith Seeking Assurance*, 154 (*Spiritual Refining*, 56).

handmaids and servants of Christ. They are but tokens from Him, not Himself. A man must not only go out of his sins but also out of his graces unto Christ....

Let not therefore your desire for inherent righteousness make you forget imputed righteousness; that is, do not take the friend of the Bridegroom for the Bridegroom Himself. Failing to do so is without doubt one reason why the people of God are so often in darkness and have no light, for they have no comfortable sign or token of God's love for them so they may stay themselves upon God.[17]

Thus, it is important to remember that the foundation of these syllogisms and their reflex actions, when properly exercised, is Christ. The believer learns to count but loss and dung all that is not Christ in order to know Him and the power of His resurrection (Phil. 3:10). Consequently, with proper self-examination, believers recognize their strengths (by the grace of God) and weaknesses (due to remaining infirmities arising from the old corrupt nature) and are driven to Christ, as Perkins said, 'that they might be all in all out of themselves in Christ'.[18]

Brooks wrote: 'We may and ought to make a sober use of characters and evidences of our gracious estates, to support, comfort, and encourage us on our way to heaven, but still in subordination to Christ, and to the fresh and frequent exercises of faith upon the person, blood, and righteousness of Jesus.'[19] These 'frequent exercises' that Brooks referred to mean that we flee by faith to Jesus not only now and then, but hundreds, even thousands of times in our lives, ever falling more in love with Him. When Christ becomes exceedingly precious to us, and like Paul, we truly regard everything else as rubbish (Phil. 3:10), it is impossible to doubt our salvation. Our communion with Christ is then like a foretaste of heaven. The Holy Spirit, through His revelation of Christ to our souls by means of the Word, stirs our affections, and through those affections that

---

17) *Faith Seeking Assurance*, 156 (*Spiritual Refining*, 57).

18) Perkins, *Works*, 2:44.

19) Brooks, *Works*, 3:237.

are grounded in Christ our own consciences testify with the Spirit's witness that we are children of God. Then we can believe both objectively and subjectively that we belong to Christ and that Christ belongs to us (see *Heidelberg Catechism*, Q. 1).

The best resolution of the objective-subjective tension in assurance is that both owe everything to Christ, receive all from Him, and end with all in Him. In Christ, objective promises and subjective experience are complementary.

Putting the Syllogisms and Reflect Act of Faith into Practice

So how does this all work in practice? Let's say that you are spiritually distressed on a given day because you feel very unspiritual, distant from God, and lukewarm in your faith. In fact, you can scarcely pray, which makes you wonder if you truly have faith at all. You turn to the Scriptures, but even special promises of God, which have been made very precious to you in the past, such as 1 John 1:9 – 'If we confess our sins, he is faithful and just to forgive us our sins, and to cleanse us from all unrighteousness' – now seem empty and distant. What do you do? Burgess and the Puritans would say that you should turn to some of the evidences of grace that are laid out for us in Scripture, ask the Spirit to shed light on them for you, and then, as you reflect on your life, if you can say with assurance that one of these evidences is your experience, you can be assured that you are a child of God – even if you can't see other evidences in you. So, for example, continuing with 1 John, you turn to 1 John 2:5, 'But whoso keepeth his word, in him verily is the love of God perfected: hereby know we that we are in him.' You then ask yourself, praying for Spirit-worked light of reflection, *Am I a keeper of Christ's Word?* Perhaps as you look at yourself, and you consider how many times you have broken God's Word and commandments recently, you need to confess on this particular day, *I'm afraid I can't see much, if anything, of that evidence of grace in me right now.* That doesn't mean you give up! Burgess would say that you should then move on to another evidence of grace. So, you keep on reading until you get to

1 John 3:14, 'We know that we have passed from death unto life, because we love the brethren.' Again, you ask yourself syllogistically, since only those who are true children of God have a true love for the brethren, do I have a true love for the people of God? Perhaps you can then answer: Yes, I certainly can't deny that I have a special love for the people of God. I love to fellowship with them; they are real brothers and sisters to me. I love to see Christ in them. Your conclusion then is: therefore, I must be a child of God.

The point is this, according to Burgess: If you can grasp one of these marks of grace (such as love for the brethren), then you may know that since God does a complete work of salvation in His people, you also possess all the other marks of grace including 1 John 2:5, even though you can't see that today. William Perkins illustrated it this way: It's like pulling one link on the bottom of a necklace; if you pull that link, there will be a tug on all the rest. In other words, you don't lose your assurance of faith because you can't find all the marks of grace in you; to the contrary, you may strengthen your assurance of faith if you can find, by the Spirit's light reflecting on your life, even one mark of grace. For then you may know that you possess all the rest of God's marks of grace and may thus be assured of your salvation, since no unbeliever can or will possess any marks of grace.

This is not to say, of course, that we should settle for minimal marks of grace in our own lives. On the contrary, those who grow in assurance most are precisely those who are growing in the marks of grace. Then, too, we must recognize that there are numerous marks of grace and of spiritual health that can be examined that are not detailed in 1 John. In his helpful book *Ten Questions to Diagnose Your Spiritual Health*, Don Whitney poses ten questions to examine ourselves with, in dependency on the Spirit, to see whether we are not only in the faith but also if we are growing in our faith in a healthy way. Just as backsliding will reduce one's level of assurance, similarly, the question of growing in assurance is, in some ways, a question of spiritual growth. John only mentions one of Whitney's questions (no. 3), but they are all sound, biblical marks of grace, and all represent areas where we need to grow: (1) Do you thirst for God? (2) Are you governed increasingly by God's Word? (3) Are you more loving? (4) Are you more sensitive to God's presence? (5) Do you have a growing concern for the spiritual and temporal needs of others? (6) Do you delight in the bride of Christ? (7) Are the spiritual disciplines increasingly important to you? (8) Do you still grieve over sin? (9) Are you a quicker forgiver? (10) Do you yearn for heaven and to be with Jesus?[20]

Thomas Brooks also provided a rather formidable list of marks of grace by which we ought to examine ourselves. These include not only graces and fruits that accompany salvation, such as spiritual knowledge, faith, repentance, obedience, love, prayer, perseverance, and hope (which he spends 115 pages on detailing!), but also six probing matters 'in which Christ's true followers are distinguished from all others': (1) Do we labor in all duties and services to be approved and accepted of God? (2) Do we labor to 'get up to the very top of holiness' – to live up to our own principles? (3) Is it our greatest desire and endeavor that sin may be cured in us rather than covered? (4) Are our souls taken up with Christ as the chief among ten thousand? (5) Are our greatest conflicts against our own inward pollutions that are obvious only to God and ourselves? (6) Are we subject to Christ as our Head?[21]

Brooks's point with these questions is not to drive us to despair, but to spur us forward to recognize even traces of God's work in us and then to strive, by the Spirit's help and witness, to grow in faith and assurance. Brooks, as well as all the Puritans, wanted to stress that the Spirit's witness with us in reflective, syllogistic assurance is an assurance that, though varying in degrees, is ongoing. It is a daily, continued, even lifelong quest and activity in the believer's soul granted by the Holy Spirit. Paul implies as much when he uses the present tense of continued activity in Romans 8:16 – 'the Spirit

---

20) Donald S. Whitney, *Ten Questions to Diagnose Your Spiritual Health* (Colorado Springs, Colo.: NavPress, 2001), 9.

21) Brooks, *Heaven on Earth*, 161–70, 173–288.

itself beareth witness'. Thus, when your spiritual life is healthy as a Christian, with the Spirit's guidance shedding light on His Word and your conscience, you will normally be able to get comfort and grow in assurance by both resorting to God's promises and by the Spirit witnessing with your spirit that you are a child of God through several, if not many, evidences of grace – at least to some degree. The more promises you can lay claim to and the more evidences of grace you can see with the Spirit's assistance as you reflect back on your life, the more assurance you will normally have. Thus, the promises of God in Christ and the evidences of grace ought to be the staple diet – the meat and potatoes – of our daily assurance for the rest of our lives.

Conclusion: Cautions Regarding Signs of Grace

Let me close with a summary of some cautions (gleaned mostly from Burgess) about using signs of grace to gain assurance.

First, be careful how you define the marks of grace. On the one hand, do not require such signs of yourself as no Christian has in this life. A true Christian keeps God's commandments (1 John 3:24), but no Christian ever comes to the point that he can say he has no sin (1 John 1:8). Although he does not hunger and thirst for God as much as he should, he does sincerely hunger and thirst for God. On the other hand, do not make signs of saving grace out of qualities that unbelievers can have. Taking the sacraments, having right doctrinal beliefs, and exercising great ability in Christian service may all appear in a person who is not born again.

Second, test your graces only by the true standard, the Word of God. Scripture alone is the light to guide our feet (Ps. 119:105); it is God's wisdom to make us wise for salvation (2 Tim. 3:15).

Third, never use the signs in a way that hinders you from receiving and applying Christ for your souls. Rest on Christ alone for reconciliation with God and atonement of your sins. Your graces are but signs of Christ; they are not Christ Himself.

Fourth, do not make signs of salvation into grounds and causes of salvation. We wrong our souls when we take pride in the evidences of God's grace in our lives and place sinful confidence in the signs. Find comfort in signs but rest in Christ. After all, our main argument before God is not something that we have done or felt, but what the triune God has already done in and through Jesus Christ.

Fifth, test yourself with signs only while simultaneously casting away your self-love and self-flattery. Many lie to themselves like the ancient Jews who cried, 'The temple of the Lord are these!' as if living in sight of the Temple guaranteed their safety and salvation. We can only know ourselves by the supernatural teaching of the Holy Spirit. At the same time, however, you must cast out your unbelief which refuses to acknowledge the work of God in your heart. How can you thank God for His grace to you if you will not acknowledge it?

Sixth, do not examine yourself for signs of grace when your soul is full of darkness, doubts, and temptations. You cannot see clearly then. It is far better at such times to cling to God's promises and to what God has done for your salvation.

Seventh, do not think that no sign will be sufficient unless you first persevere to the end. Some insist that no one can be sure of his election by God until he has persevered in faith and obedience. Thus no man can be happy until he dies. Perseverance is a promise to the godly (Phil. 1:6), but it is not the only distinctive sign of true godliness.

Eighth, when you examine yourself, pray to God for His Spirit to enlighten your eyes. The Spirit of God is the effective cause of assurance. Just as only the Spirit can bring biblical truth home to the soul, so you can have all kinds of evidence of grace but your heart will not be persuaded until the Spirit establishes you in certainty.

Ninth, never think that a person may not take hold of Christ until he has this certainty by signs of grace within himself. Do not look for spiritual qualifications before trusting Christ for your justification. Though it is popular to say that faith is a strong persuasion that my sins are forgiven, in reality justifying faith is not assurance. Assurance is a fruit of faith.

Tenth, when you, in dependency on the Spirit, examine yourself for marks of saving faith, do not begin with all kinds of marks, but begin with the foundational mark: faith itself – and then branch out from there to look at the marks that faith produces, such as love for the brethren, humility, keeping God's commandments, etc. It is good to look first for faith itself because faith is foundational to the Christian life and sometimes the act of faith itself is more discernible than any other grace. Ask yourself: Do I know something experientially of what the Reformers and especially the Puritans called *the three acts of faith*?

(1) Am a experientially acquainted with a saving *knowledge* of faith by which I obtain a spiritual sight of the beauty and glory of Christ in the gospel, by which I understand that I am saved only by His passive obedience paying for my sins and His active obedience in obeying the law perfectly on my behalf so that God can 'be just, and the justifier of him which believeth in Jesus' (Rom. 3:26)? Has the Spirit shone the supernatural 'light' of the gospel into my soul by means of the read and preached Word of God to show me that Christ is a full, glorious, and wonderful Savior (2 Cor. 4:6)?

(2) Am I experientially acquainted with a saving *assent* of faith whereby I wholeheartedly agree with, say amen to, and am committed to God's gospel truths and terms of salvation – that salvation is all through His Word alone, by grace and faith alone, in Christ alone, and to His glory alone?

(3) Am I experientially acquainted with a saving *trust* in the triune God and His gospel of salvation, such that I truly rest in Jesus Christ and His finished righteousness as a compellingly full, rich, and glorious Savior for my needy soul? For example, do my prayers reveal that I trust in Him alone even as I earnestly pray that I might know Him better – better in His person, His states, His natures, His offices, His work, His love, His glory?

In fact, even the yearning to know Christ better is already, at least implicitly, an act of faith. After William Perkins once listed numerous marks of faith, he concluded by saying that if his reader was still in doubt about whether he possessed faith or not, he would provide one more mark of grace that no believing reader could deny: *Do you long to know Christ better?* Do you find such beauty in Christ as to desire Him (Isa. 53:2)? True faith always makes us long to have Christ for ourselves and to know Him better.[22]

Last, do not resist God's Spirit with unbelief when He comes to assure you with evidences of your salvation. It is a great sin to rebel against the Spirit when He convinces a person of sin, but it is a greater sin to resist Him when He moves us to claim God as our Father, for His greatest glory lies in being the Spirit of adoption (Rom. 8:15; Gal. 4:6).[23]

---

22) Cf. John Piper, 'The Agonizing Problem of the Assurance of Salvation' – a letter posted on April 28, 1998, on the Desiring God website.

23) The last section of this chapter, and some of the material summarizing Burgess in the previous two chapters, has been revised from Joel Beeke and Paul Smalley, 'Assurance of Salvation: The Insights of Anthony Burgess', *Puritan Reformed Journal* 6, no. 2 (July 2014): 171–84.

❧ 7 ❧

Assurance from the Holy Spirit's Witnessing Testimony

The *Westminster Confession*, 18.2, teaches us that we gain our assurance as Christians not only by casting ourselves on the promises and by the Spirit-worked perception of the evidences of God's saving work within us, but also by the witnessing testimony of the Holy Spirit Himself, or in the words of the Confession:

> ...the testimony of the Spirit of adoption witnessing with our spirits that we are the children of God, which Spirit is the earnest of our inheritance, whereby we are sealed to the day of redemption.

The Spirit's Witness

The writers of the *Westminster Confession* knew that the most difficult part of assurance to understand was the testimony or witness of the Holy Spirit. They confessed that vast mysteries confronted them when they spoke of that subject. No doubt one reason the assembly did not detail more specifically the Spirit's role in assurance was to allow for the freedom of the Spirit. A second reason was that the assembly wanted to allow freedom of conscience to those who differed about the finer details of the Spirit's testimony. Most of the members of the assembly had one of two emphases. Some believed that the Spirit's witness referred to in *Westminster Confession* 18.2 was simply the Spirit witnessing with our spirit that the inward

107

evidences of grace are true so that we may be assured that we are children of God. Thus, nothing more was intended here than what we already covered in the last chapter. According to these divines, there is then only one secondary ground of assurance: the evidences of grace, co-witnessed with our spirits by the Spirit of God.

Other Puritans said that though that may be part of the meaning here, there can also be a direct witness of the Holy Spirit to the believer's soul through the Word that can give a substantial increase to his assurance and comfort, especially in times of great need. For example, when the Spirit applies to the soul a special promise such as, 'I have loved thee with an everlasting love: therefore with lovingkindness have I drawn thee' (Jer. 31:3), with considerable power and sweetness – such that the believer enjoys a profound experience of communion with God and of His love and a profound sight of the beauty and glory of Christ – that immediate or direct witness of the Spirit to the believer can give a large boost to his or her assurance. At such times, the believer feels that the intimately personal application of the Word to his soul seems to be the most suitable text in the entire Bible for his particular need. J. I. Packer describes this view of some Puritans as follows:

> This is a direct and immediate sense of God's fatherly love given as kind of an immediate communication – like God is saying 'I love you' – directly, immediately to the soul through His Word. It is like a father saying to his child, 'I love you,' as a good parent sometimes does. So with God and His children, the Spirit, who comes in as the Spirit of adoption, mediates to us these high moments, this thrilling realization that God is, as it were, saying to my soul, 'I am your salvation; I am your father; I love you.'[1]

If you've experienced this kind of direct testimony of the Holy Spirit, you know what it means to have such an application of the Word grip you, overwhelm you, master you, and make you bow in submission before the triune God. It bolsters assurance within you,

---

1) J. I. Packer, notes from a conference address, 'The Puritan View of Sanctification (3): Assurance and Conduct'.

and both strengthens and humbles you in every way internally even though no external circumstance may have changed in your life. You acquiesce to whatever trial you are going through, and you embrace the Lord with joy and with freedom. You find yourself repeating that text a hundred times or more. That text becomes so sweet to you; you cling to it, plead it, and pray over it; it becomes 'sweeter than honey and the honeycomb' (Ps. 19:10). It bears fruit in your life, augmenting God's graces within you.

Burgess held the first opinion. He emphasized that the Spirit's witness coincides with assurance gleaned from the evidences of grace, which he identifies as evidences of sanctification or fruits of holiness. He asked, 'Is the work of God's Spirit in us through sanctification the only witness to our salvation, or is there also an immediate testimony of God's Spirit to the soul apart from the gracious fruits of holiness?' He answered, 'I believe the fruits of holiness are the only safe and sure witness of sanctification, which, for the most part, Scripture commends.'[2] By calling the evidences of grace 'the only safe and sure witness', Burgess implied that he did not want to admit that the direct testimony of the Holy Spirit was a safe form of assurance. Burgess and some other Puritans believed that if the immediate or direct testimony of the Spirit was embraced as a distinct form of assurance it would tend to promote mysticism by exalting experience for its own sake and might also promote antinomianism by downplaying the need to produce practical fruits of faith and repentance.[3]

Westminster divines Jeremiah Burroughs and George Gillespie agreed with Burgess.[4] They said the witnessing testimony of the

---

2) *Faith Seeking Assurance*, 122 (*Spiritual Refining*, 44).

3) *Faith Seeking Assurance*, 144 (*Spiritual Refining*, 52). A classic case of someone who abused the direct testimony of the Spirit so as to promote antinomian assurance was Anne Hutchinson (1591–1643), who was an outspoken and controversial figure whose views disturbed the peace of the Massachusetts Bay Colony.

4) Jeremiah Burroughs, *The Saints' Happiness, together with the several steps leading thereunto. Delivered in Divers Lectures on the Beatitudes* (reprint ed.,

Holy Spirit in assurance referred exclusively to His activity in conjunction with the syllogisms certifying the believer's evidences of grace, whereby He brings conscience to unite with His witness that the Christian is a child of God. According to this view, the witness of the Holy Spirit conjoins *with* the witness of the believer's spirit. Romans 8:15 and 8:16 are thus synonymous: 'For ye have not received the spirit of bondage again to fear; but ye have received the Spirit of adoption, whereby we cry, Abba, Father. The Spirit itself beareth witness with our spirit, that we are the children of God.' Burgess wrote, 'The meaning is that the Spirit of God bears witness to us with those gifts and graces that are the fruit of the Spirit. Thus the apostle speaks not of such an immediate [that is, direct] testimony... but mediately [that is, through means] by and with our spirits, which are enlightened and sanctified, so that though the Spirit of God be the only author of this assurance, yet it is in an ordinary way made evident by the fruits of the Spirit.'[5] He likewise interpreted the sealing 'with the Holy Spirit of promise' in Ephesians 1:13. He wrote, 'Those who understand this sealing as the extraordinary and miraculous gifts of God's Spirit do not hit the mark because these are not necessary signs of adoption. Also, they are not bestowed upon every particular believer. We must therefore view sealing as one of the sanctifying graces of God's Spirit.... Thus does God the Father seal His children by furnishing them with all the graces of His Holy Spirit, for by these they know they are of God.'[6]

Burgess believed the secondary grounds of assurance did not break down into two kinds because the inward evidences of grace and the testimony of the Spirit are essentially one. If this were not so and the believer received assurance through the direct testimony of the Spirit, then there would be no need to pursue assurance through

---

Beaver Falls, Pa.: Soli Deo Gloria, 1988), 196; George Gillespie, *A Treatise of Miscellany Questions* (Edinburgh: Gedeon Lithgow, for George Swintuun, 1649), 105–9.

5) *Faith Seeking Assurance*, 136–7 (*Spiritual Refining*, 49).

6) *Faith Seeking Assurance*, 138 (*Spiritual Refining*, 50).

inward graces, for such a pursuit would be 'as useless as lighting a candle when the sun is shining. Yet both are necessary, for the testimony of the Spirit and the evidence of graces make up one complete witness. They are therefore not to be disjoined.'[7] Thus, for Burgess, Spirit-enlightened syllogisms based on inward evidences of grace meant full assurance.

Other divines of the assembly such as Samuel Rutherford, William Twisse, Henry Scudder, and Thomas Goodwin presented another emphasis. They said the witness of the Spirit described in Romans 8:15 contains something distinct from that of verse 16.[8] They distinguished the Spirit witnessing *with* the believer's spirit by syllogism from His witnessing *to* the believer's spirit by direct applications of the Word. As the New Testament commentator Heinrich Meyer showed, the former leaves in its wake the self-conscious conviction '*I* am a child of God' and, on the basis of such Spirit-worked syllogisms, finds freedom to approach God as Father. The latter speaks the Spirit's pronouncement on behalf of the Father, '*You* are a child of God', and, on the basis of hearing of its sonship from God's own Word by the Spirit, approaches Him with the familiarity of a child.[9]

Those who accepted two secondary grounds of assurance differed as to whether the Spirit's direct testimony should be regarded as more valuable than His syllogistic testimony and hence be placed practically on a higher level. Thomas Goodwin, for example, asserted that the direct witness of the Spirit supersedes the co-witnessing

---

7) *Faith Seeking Assurance*, 132 (*Spiritual Refining*, 47–8).

8) Samuel Rutherford, *The Covenant of Life Opened* (Edinburgh: Andrew Anderson for Robert Broun, 1655), 65–7; William Twisse, *The Doctrine of the Synod of Dort and Arles* (Amsterdam: G. Thorpe, 1631), 147–9; Henry Scudder, *The Christian's Daily Walk* (reprint, Harrisonburg, Va.: Sprinkle, 1984), 338–42; Goodwin, *Works*, 6:27; 7:66; 8:351, 363.

9) Henrich Meyer, *Critical and Exegetical Hand-book to The Epistle of the Romans* (New York: Funk & Wagnalls, 1889), 316. Cf. Robert Bolton, *Some General Directions for a Comfortable Walking with God* (Morgan, Pa.: Soli Deo Gloria, 1995), 326.

of the Spirit and the believer through the syllogisms.[10] Generally speaking, however, other Westminster divines did not view the direct testimony of the Spirit as superior to or independent of the syllogisms but as added to them. They agreed that the syllogistic way of reaching assurance is more common and safe than seeking immediate assurance by the Spirit's direct witness. For example, Rutherford said the reflex act of faith is as a rule 'more spiritual and helpful' than direct acts.[11] Burgess, giving some allowance for the second emphasis under certain conditions, put it this way: If the direct testimony be allowed, it is 'more subject to dangerous delusions', for the reflex act 'is founded upon a [more] sure ground, the fruits of mortification and vivification'[12] – that is, the fruits of putting off or killing the old nature and of putting on or quickening the new nature (Col. 3:7-13). But other Puritans stressed that the Spirit's direct or immediate testimony also bore such fruits – in fact, that it is precisely such fruit-bearing that reveals whether such experiences were truly the work of the Holy Spirit. If such fruit is lacking, such experiences are not flowing from the saving ministry of the Spirit.

Burgess summarized the view of those Puritans who differed in emphasis when he stated, 'Some divines do not deny the possibility of God's immediate testimony, but they conclude that the ordinary and safe way is to look for the testimony which is evident in the effects and fruits of God's Spirit.'[13] Most of the assembly's divines agreed that regardless of what you believe about the direct witness of the Spirit, it is hard to see that it is the most important kind of assurance, for Christians are called to live daily in the joy of assurance, and such assurance cannot be maintained on the basis of occasional experiences.

---

10) Goodwin, *Works*, 1:233; 8:366.

11) *Catechism of the Second Reformation*, ed. Alexander Mitchell (London: Nisbet, 1866), 207; Samuel Rutherford, *The Trial and Triumph of Faith* (Edinburgh: Collins, 1845), 88–90.

12) *Faith Seeking Assurance*, 173 (*Spiritual Refining*, 672).

13) *Faith Seeking Assurance*, 144 (*Spiritual Refining*, 52).

In every sense, however, the assembly's divines unitedly asserted that the Spirit's testimony is always tied to, and may never contradict, the Word of God. Only then can antinomianism be avoided, they said, and the freedom of the Spirit be protected.

For most of the Westminster divines, all the grounds of faith in God's promises, inward evidences of grace realized through syllogisms, and the witness of the Spirit must be pursued to obtain as full a measure of assurance as possible. If any of these grounds are emphasized at the expense of others, the pursuit of assurance loses balance and becomes dangerous. No Puritan would teach that assurance is obtainable by trusting only in the promises, or only in inward evidences, or only in the direct witnessing testimony of the Holy Spirit. Rather, they taught that the believer cannot truly trust the promises without the aid of the Holy Spirit, and that he cannot with any degree of safety examine himself without the illumination of the Spirit.

Burgess taught that two graces ought to be joined together in believers: 'They are to believe firmly on God's promise, and yet to be humble in themselves. They are to rejoice, and yet with trembling. When your confidence devours your holy trembling, then take heed of presumption. When your fear devours your faith and joy, then take heed of despair.... One cannot work without the other.'[14] Although Burgess and most of his Puritan colleagues gave the syllogisms a significant role in assurance, nearly all of them regarded the promises of God as the primary ground for assurance.[15]

The activity of the Spirit is essential in every part of assurance. As Burgess said, 'As a man by the power of free will is not able to do any supernatural good thing, so neither by the strength of natural light can he discern the gracious privileges God bestows

---

14) Anthony Burgess, *CXLV Expository Sermons upon the whole 17th Chapter of the Gospel According to St. John: or Christ's Prayer Before his Passion Explication, and both Practically and Polemically Improved* (London: Abraham Miller for Thomas Underhill, 1656), 356.

15) Graafland, 'Van *syllogismus practicus* naar *syllogismus mysticus*', 108, 120; *Faith Seeking Assurance*, 139 (*Spiritual Refining*, 52).

upon him (1 Cor. 2:12).'[16] Without the application of the Spirit, the promises of God lead to self-deceit, carnal presumption, and fruitless lives. Without the illumination of the Spirit, self-examination tends to introspection, bondage, and legalism. The witness of the Spirit, divorced from the promises of God and from scriptural inward evidences, can lead to unbiblical mysticism and excessive emotionalism.

Practical Use of the Spirit's Direct Testimony

I have thought long and hard for more than three decades about this debate on the validity of the Spirit's direct testimony. I believe that Rutherford's, Twisse's, and Scudder's view – who take the middle road between Goodwin (who tends to exaggerate its importance) and Burgess (who tends to minimize it) – is the safest and surest way to interpret this phenomenon with regard to assurance. Let me explain.

Practically speaking, it is not wise to deny the Spirit's direct testimony as part of the doctrine of assurance, as that would be to deny the very genuine experience of many of God's children.[17] Allow me to use my own experience, which I am confident that many believers can identify with in a variety of ways according to God's sovereign leading in their lives. When I was fourteen years old, the Holy Spirit brought me under deep conviction of sin. For eighteen months, I found little relief. Much of that time I feared I was a reprobate destined for hell. At the very least, I knew I fully deserved hell. Sometimes I hardly dared to walk on the grass, for fear that the earth would swallow me up like Korah, Dathan, and Abiram (Num. 16:23-35). I knew I needed a Savior, but I didn't know how to find Him or embrace Him. I searched the Scriptures and read my father's entire bookcase of Puritan writers, often reading until early morning hours. Sometimes I received a bit of comfort and

---

16) Burgess, *The True Doctrine of Iustification*, 273. Cf. chapter 10 below.

17) For a more exegetical defense of this position based on Romans 8:12-17, see chapter 10 below.

hope, but more commonly, salvation just seemed impossible for me. I hated sin, loved God, longed for His fellowship, but felt I either lacked saving faith altogether or had so little of it that I certainly lacked all assurance of faith. At times, I felt I could cry out with the demoniac's father in Mark 9:24, 'Lord, I believe; help thou mine unbelief.' At other times, I could get no comfort whatsoever from God's promises nor from searching for inward evidences of grace.

At about that time, we finally received a minister in the church in which I was reared. The minister wanted to meet every family in the church by gathering entire family circles together. The evening he met our family he ended up dialoguing with my grandfather who was a true child of God but had struggled with the question of assurance for most of his life. Part way through the discussion, the minister said to him quite authoritatively, 'For you, too, my friend, there is a way of escape in Christ Jesus!'

The Holy Spirit took those Bible-based words and applied them directly to my heart with an overwhelming power. The words the minister intended for my grandfather were blessed to me. Immediately I could believe sweetly and fully for the first time in my life that Jesus Christ had paid for my sins by His sufferings and death (His passive obedience) and had fully obeyed the law on my behalf (His active obedience), so that through this double obedience, God could be just and justify me at the same time as I believed in Jesus Christ alone for salvation (cf. Rom. 3:24-6). I didn't know the terms passive and active obedience at that time, but I experienced with a profound sense of relief that Jesus was now my Savior and Lord based on these two things that He had done for me. As impossible as it was before this blessed evening for me to say with assurance, 'Jesus died for me and is my Savior', so impossible it was for me now to deny that He died for me and was my Savior. My burden of sin was lifted off my heart and my shoulders and I was overwhelmed with joy. I went to bed that night a free young man in Christ Jesus. The joy of salvation I experienced that night I will never be able to forget. Fifty years later it is nearly as vivid for me now as it was then. It was as if God spoke to me as a

Father, saying, 'I forgive you all your sins and love you as My child; I am your salvation, I am your Father, I love you for Jesus's sake.' I couldn't stop weeping tears of joy until 3:00 a.m. when I finally awoke my father to tell him that I had been saved by the powerful substitutionary work of Jesus Christ applied to my soul by the Holy Spirit for the forgiveness of all my sins.

Since then, I have also had several times in my life when a particular promise from Scripture was applied to my soul with a degree of comfort and power combined with a sense of the love of and communion with God and the beauty and fullness of Christ, such that I could not deny it was the work of the Holy Spirit sweetly comforting me through His Word. On a few other special occasions in my life, just the felt presence of the Holy Spirit applying truth to my soul that was not necessarily connected with a particular promise has given a real boost to my assurance. Richard Sibbes described this sweet experience well: 'The Spirit doth not always witness unto us our condition by force of argument from sanctification, but sometimes immediately by way of presence; as the sight of a friend comforts without discourse.'[18] The soul-enlarging, comforting joy of the internal presence of the Holy Spirit known and felt at such special times in our lives cannot be put into human words; when He takes the things of Christ and reveals them directly to us through the Word with an unusual degree of power, we may know a peace that passes all understanding.

Have you ever felt the Spirit's indwelling presence within you in a soul-enlarging measure? Perhaps you were discouraged, but you felt His presence grant you a gracious reviving. Perhaps you were weak or faint or sick, but you felt His presence impart strength and lift you up. Perhaps you felt deserted, but He was there to arouse you to fervent prayer. Perhaps you were deeply distressed, but He ministered divine consolation to your heart. O the blessedness of the indwelling Spirit who testifies that He resides in us for one

---

18) Richard Sibbes, *Works of Richard Sibbes* (Edinburgh: Banner of Truth Trust, 1973), 5:440.

very good reason – by grace and through faith we belong to God! Every time we may feel His presence, it is a humbling, assuring, and compelling testimony of God's grace and of our life of faith in the triune God.

Each of these special occasions in my life gave me an extra boost to my degree of assurance and humbled me in the dust before God. I firmly believe that such experiences as these are also the testimony of the Holy Spirit applying His own Word of truth directly to the soul. In his exposition of Romans, James Boice confirmed what I am saying in a balanced way:

> I am convinced [that Romans 8:16] teaches that there is such a thing as a direct witness of the Holy Spirit to believers that they are sons or daughters of God, even apart from the other 'proofs' I have mentioned. In other words, it is possible to have a genuine *experience* of the Holy Spirit in one's heart. Experience the Spirit? I know the objections. I know that no spiritual experience is ever necessarily valid in itself. Any such experience can be counterfeited, and the devil's counterfeits can be very good indeed. But the fact that a spiritual experience can be counterfeited does not invalidate all of them. I also know that those who seek experiences of the Holy Spirit frequently run to excess and fall into unbiblical ideas and practices. Every such experience must be tested by Scripture. But in spite of these objections, which are important, I still say that there can be a direct experience of the Spirit that is valid testimony to the fact that one is truly God's child. Haven't you ever had such an experience? An overwhelming sense of God's presence? Or haven't you at some point, perhaps at many points in your life, been aware that God has come upon you in a special way and that there is no doubt whatever that what you are experiencing is from God? You may have been moved to tears. You may have deeply felt some other sign of God's presence, by which you were certainly moved to a greater and more wonderful love for him.[19]

In forty years of ministry, I have met hundreds of Christians who have had similar experiences as mine and those that James Boice

---

19) James Montgomery Boice, *Romans* (Grand Rapids: Baker, 1992), 2:843–4.

described, but I have also met hundreds of Christians who have not had these kinds of experiences. They often can affirm that they know of a co-witnessing work of the Spirit with their spirit that they are children of God through a reflex act of faith, but do not seem to know of a direct testimony of the Spirit to their soul through the Word with comforting, joyous, and humbling power. What are we to make of this? How are we to put a fence around such experiences so as to avoid the problems of mysticism or antinomianism as we saw above that Burgess feared? Here are four helps:

First, do not make too much of these experiences. The main thing in the Christian life is to walk every day in God's promises and precepts. Iain Murray put it this way, 'Whatever we say about the direct and immediate witness of the Spirit, it is hard to see that it is the most important, for we are called to live daily in the joy of assurance, and such continued assurance cannot be made to depend upon very occasional and intermittent experiences.'[20]

I like to put it this way: assurance that comes by the general promises of God in Christ Jesus and by the regular way of examining evidences of grace in one's soul and life through the Spirit's Word-based light are the meat and potatoes of daily assurance. Assurance received through the direct testimony of the Spirit powerfully applied to the soul is like an occasional rich dessert, but is in no way superior to the daily diet. Though these experiences do augment the believer's assurance, having such experiences does not make a Christian any higher or better than another Christian. That is critical to maintain – otherwise, we could well fall into a kind of experientialism where our eyes are taken off Christ and end up focusing only on our experiences.

Second, such experiences must be tested by the Word of God to avoid false mysticism (Isa. 8:20). If such experiences are merely emotional they will not be grounded in the truths of God's Word. In the experience I related above, however, the truth that Christ

---

20) Personal correspondence, February 25, 1989; cf. Beeke, *Assurance of Faith: Calvin, English Puritanism, and the Dutch Second Reformation*, 204, n.153.

is a way of escape for the greatest of sinners is eminently biblical (1 Tim. 1:15) and hence does not smack of false mysticism.

Third, such experiences must be tested by the fruits of our lives to avoid antinomianism (Matt. 7:16). If these kinds of experiences produce the fruits of the Spirit as recorded in Galatians 5:22, 23 (love, joy, peace, longsuffering, gentleness, goodness, faith, meekness, and temperance) and the fruits of the Beatitudes in Matthew 5:3-12 (poverty of spirit, mourning over sin, meekness, hungering and thirsting after righteousness, mercifulness, purity of heart, peacemaking, and being persecuted for righteousness's sake), we may know that these fruits coalesce with the fruits of the inward evidences of the Spirit, and therefore they were genuine testimonies of the Holy Spirit. If, however, the fruit of such experiences is a careless and presumptive lifestyle, and a kind of high-minded attitude of superiority over other Christians, you can be sure that these experiences were not the Holy Spirit's work.

Assurance in all kinds – be it through the promises of God, inward evidences of grace, or by the direct testimony of the Spirit – always bears God-honoring fruits. It produces holy living marked by spiritual peace, joyful love, humble gratitude, and cheerful obedience.

Last, such experiences also involve the testimony of the Holy Spirit witnessing with our spirit that we are the children of God. This is made abundantly clear by the *Canons of Dort* (1618–1619), written nearly thirty years prior to the *Westminster Confession*. Though using slightly different language, Head 5, Article 10 of the Canons provides the same primary ground of assurance and the same two secondary grounds of assurance as the *Westminster Confession* would present (according to the views of Rutherford and Goodwin) when it says, 'This assurance, however, is not produced by any peculiar revelation contrary to, or independent of the Word of God, but springs [1] from faith in God's promises, which He has most abundantly revealed in His Word for our comfort, [2] from the testimony of the Holy Spirit witnessing with our spirit that we are children and heirs of God (Rom. 8:16), and [3] lastly, from a serious and holy desire to preserve a good conscience and to perform good works' – which is another way of saying 'evidences of grace'.

The similarity of thought is so striking between the earlier *Canons of Dort* and the later *Westminster Confession* that one is tempted to think that the Westminster divines leaned heavily on the Canons in their own formulation. But of this we can by no means be sure since many divines in both the British and Continental traditions pinpoint the identical three grounds of assurance in their writings from the late sixteenth century onward. It is interesting to note that whereas the *Westminster Confession*, 18.2, left its language a bit vague on making a sharp distinction between the two secondary grounds of assurance so that divines who believed either in one or two secondary grounds of assurance could freely support the language, the *Canons of Dort* make clear that there are two secondary grounds of assurance – one more direct [see no. 2 above] and one more reflexive [see no. 3 above], but both depending on the testimony of the Holy Spirit witnessing with our spirits that we are the children of God.

8

How to Cultivate Assurance

The godly farmer who plows his field, sows seed, fertilizes, and cultivates is acutely aware that in the final analysis he is utterly dependent for a crop on forces outside of himself. He knows he cannot cause the seed to germinate, the rain to fall, the sun to shine. But he pursues his task with diligence anyhow, both looking to God for blessing and knowing that if he does not fertilize and cultivate the sown seed his crop will be meager at best.

Similarly, the Christian seeking to grow in assurance must be like a cultivated field to produce the fruits of holy living unto God, for he knows that if he persists in low levels of holiness and obedience he will most likely stagnate, at best, with low levels of assurance. First Thessalonians 4:7 says, 'God hath not called us unto uncleanness, but unto holiness.' And Hebrews 12:14 states categorically, 'Follow peace with all men, and holiness, without which no man shall see the Lord.' The believer who does not cultivate holiness diligently will neither have much genuine assurance of his own salvation nor be in obedience to Peter's call to seek it (2 Pet. 1:10).

But just how do you make 'your calling and election sure'? How do you cultivate assurance? That's the burden of *Westminster Confession*, 18.3:

> This infallible assurance doth not so belong to the essence of faith, but that a true believer may wait long, and conflict with many difficulties,

before he be partaker of it: yet, being enabled by the Spirit to know the things which are freely given him of God, he may, without extraordinary revelation, in the right use of ordinary means, attain thereunto. And therefore it is the duty of every one to give all diligence to make his calling and election sure, that thereby his heart may be enlarged in peace and joy in the Holy Ghost, in love and thankfulness to God, and in strength and cheerfulness in the duties of obedience, the proper fruits of this assurance; so far is it from inclining men to looseness.

Five practical issues on assurance are explained in 18.3 of the *Westminster Confession*: the relation of faith to assurance, the time that may be involved in attaining assurance, the means of attaining assurance, the duty of pursuing assurance, and the fruits produced by assurance. Let's look at each of these in turn.

The Relation of Faith to Assurance

The opening lines of *Westminster Confession* 18.3 have caused considerable debate: 'This infallible assurance doth not so belong to the essence of faith, but that a true believer may wait long, and conflict with many difficulties, before he be partaker of it.' English, Scottish, and Dutch theologians have written much about the Confession's assertion that assurance does not belong to the essence of faith. Some critics argue against it, saying the Confession denies an organic relationship between faith and assurance. As evidence, they cite question 81 of the *Larger Catechism*, which includes the words, 'Assurance of grace and salvation not being of the essence of faith...'. These critics fail to recognize that in this context the Confession speaks of assurance in the sense of faith's well-being, not of its essence or being, which must necessarily include assurance.[1]

A commonly debated question in church history is this: Is the seed of assurance embedded in faith? Most Puritans and

---

1) Brooks, *Works*, 2:371. Cf. Louis Berkhof, *Assurance of Faith* (Grand Rapids: Smitter Book Co., 1928), 27–9, 43–4; James Buchanan, *The Doctrine of Justification* (1867; reprint, Grand Rapids: Baker, 1977), 185, 378; Alexander M'Leod, *The Life and Power of True Godliness* (New York: Eastburn, 1816), 246–7.

their contemporary Scottish divines argued yes. And yet they distinguished faith from assurance of faith. 'It is one thing for me to believe, and another thing for me to believe that I believe', said Brooks.[2] William Ames (1576–1633) added, 'It also appears that assurance of salvation is not, properly speaking, justifying faith but a fruit of such faith.'[3]

This distinction between faith and assurance has profound doctrinal and pastoral implications. To make justification dependent upon assurance compels a believer to rely upon his own spiritual condition rather than on the sufficiency of the triune God in redemption. Self-reliance is not only unsound doctrine but also has adverse pastoral effects. God does not require full and perfect faith, but He does require sincere, genuine faith. The fulfillment of God's promises depends on receiving Christ's righteousness, not upon the degree of assurance in that act.[4] The smallest spark of faith is as valid as assured faith in terms of salvation. 'Neither are we saved by the worth or quantity of our faith, but by Christ, which is laid hold of by a weak faith, as well as a strong' faith, wrote John Rogers (c. 1570–1636).[5] If salvation depends on full assurance of faith, many believers would despair, for then 'the palsied hand of faith should not receive Christ', said John Downame (d. 1652).[6]

Most Puritans did not deny there was some assurance in every exercise of faith, however, so they could say that all believers possess at least some assurance at times. 'There be Christians of all ages and

---

2) Brooks, *Heaven on Earth*, 14.

3) William Ames, *The Marrow of Theology*, trans. John Eusden (1629; reprint, Boston: Pilgrim Press, 1968), 167 (I.xxviii.24).

4) John Ball, *A Treatise of Faith* (London: Robert Young for Edward Brewster, 1637), 84–7.

5) John Rogers, *The Doctrine of Faith: wherein are particularly handled twelve Principall Points, which explaine the Nature and Vse of it* (London: N. Newbery and H. Overton, 1629), 201.

6) John Downame, *A Treatise of the True Nature and Definition of Justifying Faith* (Oxford: I. Lichfield for E. Forrest, 1635), 12–13.

of all sizes in God's family,' wrote Robert Harris; 'all God's children have some assurance, though all have not alike.'[7]

Assurance grows organically out of faith like a plant out of a seed, or a flower grows out of a plant and a root. Assurance then pertains to one's present degree of faith. Ames wrote, 'Believers do not have the same assurance of grace and favor of God, nor do the same ones have it at all times.'[8] Richard Hawkes rightly notes, 'While the Puritans distinguish full assurance from the initial trust of faith, they will not allow a division between the two, for full assurance grows out of an assurance implicit in the first act of faith.'[9] Thus Puritan divines could speak of assurance growing out of faith as well as of faith growing into assurance. For example, Brooks wrote, 'Faith, in time, will of its own accord raise and advance itself to assurance.'[10]

But the Puritans usually focus on full assurance rather than the small but growing element of assurance present in faith from its conception. They differentiate between the faith of adherence to Christ and the faith of assurance (or evidence) in Christ, whereby the believer knows that Christ has died specifically for him.[11] According to Anthony Burgess, 'Faith of adherence is many times where this faith of evidence is not.... [By sin we often] chase away

---

7) Robert Harris, *The Way to True Happinesse* (London: I. Bartlett, 1632), 2:51.

8) William Ames, *Medvlla S. S. Theologiae, ex sacris literis, earumque inter-pretibus, extracta & methodicè disposita* (Amstelodami: Joannem Janssonium, 1627), 1.27.19.

9) Richard Hawkes, 'The Logic of Assurance in English Puritan Theology', 250.

10) Brooks, *Heaven on Earth*, 15, 21. John Dod and Robert Cleaver distinguished between 'moon-shine' assurance given upon assenting to and trusting in the promise and 'sun-shine' assurance attained with 'full assurance' (*A Plaine and Familiar Exposition of the The Ten Commandements*, 1603), 10.

11) Ames, *Medvlla*, 1.27.16; Ball, *A Treatise of Faith*, 90ff.; Robert Bolton, *Some General Directions for a Comfortable Walking with God* (London: Felix Kyngston, 1625), 321–2; John Preston, *The Breast-Plate of Faith and Love*, 5th ed. (London: W. I. for Nicholas Bourne, 1632), part 1, 63–4.

our assurance; many times the people of God may walk without this comfortable persuasion' of the faith of evidence.[12]

Though some Puritan writings speak of assurance as the mature confidence that one is a child of God and other writings speak of assurance as something present in all faith, the organic relationship between faith and assurance shows this is not a great theological difference. As John Rogers said, 'The greatest Giant was in swaddling clothes, the tallest oak was a twig, and faith grows from a grain of mustard seed to a tall tree.'[13] The context of the Puritan writing being examined usually determines whether the author is speaking of assurance embedded in faith in seed form or a fulsome kind of conscious assurance that belongs to a mature faith.

Anne Dutton (1692–1765), an English poet and Calvinist Baptist writer with remarkable spiritual depth, expressed this Puritan conviction well in a personal letter to John Wesley. She argued against taking 'nothing to be faith but full assurance, or a full assurance of interest in Christ's great salvation', saying:

> Though I grant that true, saving faith has assurance in its essence or nature, and more or less in its actings, yet this assurance is latent or lies hid, as it were, in the first actings of faith, and is not sensibly discerned or felt by the soul until faith arrives at a greater strength.... I believe that it is generally experienced by the saints that in their first actings of faith, their assurance is rather an assurance of the saving object than of their own salvation.... [In this way,] faith is separable from assurance; or, faith in its first actings is previous to assurance.[14]

The Time Involved in Attaining Assurance

Sinclair Ferguson writes, 'Experiencing assurance can be complex for the simple reason that we ourselves are deeply complex individuals; there may be much in our natural psyche that militates against

---

12) Burgess, *Spiritual Refining*, 672.

13) Rogers, *The Doctrine of Faith*, 200.

14) Anne Dutton, letter to John Wesley, in *Selected Spiritual Writings of Anne Dutton* (Macon, Ga.: Mercer University Press, 2002), 1:25–7.

assurance. It may take time before we who are loved know that we are truly loved, and it may take time before we who are forgiven understand and enjoy that we are indeed forgiven.'[15]

According to the *Westminster Confession* 'a true believer may wait long, and conflict with many difficulties, before he be partaker of assurance' (18.3), but the relationship between faith and assurance usually strengthens over time, 'growing up in many to the attainment of a full assurance' (14.3). The acorn of faith will often evolve into the oak of full assurance. At the beginning, faith may bring forth only thirtyfold, but with the Spirit providing and blessing the proper nourishment, faith will frequently produce a hundredfold (Matt. 13:8).

Grace usually grows with age, and as faith increases, other graces increase. Young believers normally display much zeal, but older saints 'grow more in strength and stableness, and are more refined', said Sibbes.[16] And Brooks wrote, 'Assurance is meat for strong men; few babes, if any, are able to bear it, and digest it.'[17] Charles Spurgeon said that some young believers make a great mistake by expecting 'ripe fruit upon a tree in spring, and because that season yields nothing but blossoms, they conclude the tree to be barren'.[18] That mistake can bring barrenness and darkness upon their own souls. Though they ought to strive for assurance, they – as well as mature saints around them – must remember that it would be very unusual for them to have a high degree of mature assurance when they are but babes in grace who have scarcely begun to learn to walk by faith rather than by sight (cf. John 9:25).

Age and experience do not guarantee assurance, however, nor is it impossible for God to plant faith and full assurance simultaneously. Spurgeon spoke on the one hand of both ministers and martyrs who lacked full assurance of faith until the very end

---

15) Ferguson, 'Reformation and Assurance', 20.

16) Sibbes, *Works*, 7:222–3.

17) Brooks, *Works*, 2:371.

18) Spurgeon, *Metropolitan Tabernacle Pulpit*, 10 (1864):549.

of their lives, and on the other hand of new 'converts who have been as certified of their interest in Christ as though they had been seventy years experimentally walking with him'.[19] As in conversion, God remains sovereign in the dispensing of assurance. Typically, however, Burgess said, 'He works it by degrees',[20] so that the believer's doubts about his own salvation generally diminish as he grows in grace (2 Pet. 1:5-10).

Finally, as George Downame noted, even the most assured Christian may grow in assurance: 'None are so perfect, but that their assurance may be increased.'[21] The believer has a lifelong call to make diligent use of the means of grace in pursuit of ever greater degrees of assurance.

The Means of Attaining Assurance

Westminster Confession 18.3 goes on to say that, 'being enabled by the Spirit to know the things which are freely given him of God, [the believer] may, without extraordinary revelation, *in the right use of ordinary means*, attain to assurance'. Burgess said the believer has a lifelong call to make diligent use of the means of grace in pursuit of ever greater degrees of assurance, because God uses both sovereignty and means to bequeath assurance.[22] Four means are predominant: God's Word, the sacraments, prayer, and affliction. These are the most common means God uses to increase assurance.

God's Word

God's Word – both law and gospel, precept and promise – read and heard, believed and obeyed, memorized and meditated on, prayed

---

19) Spurgeon, *Metropolitan Tabernacle Pulpit*, 10 (1864):558.

20) Burgess, *The True Doctrine of Iustification*, 152.

21) George Downame, *The Covenant of Grace* (Dublin: Society of Stationers, 1631), 109.

22) Anthony Burgess, *CXLV Expository Sermons upon the Whole 17th Chapter of the Gospel according to St. John* (London: Abraham Miller for Thomas Underhill, 1656), 356.

and sung, is God's primary road to holiness, spiritual growth, and assurance of faith. That's why Peter advises, 'Desire the sincere milk of the word, that ye may grow thereby' (1 Pet. 2:2).

If you would grow in assurance, read through the Bible habitually. Even more importantly, memorize the Scriptures (Ps. 119:11), search (John 5:39) and meditate upon them (Ps. 1:2), live and love them (Pss. 19:10; 119), and listen to sermons of faithful preachers on the Lord's Day and during the week. Compare Scripture with Scripture; take time to study the Word. Proverbs 2:1-5 sets before us the following principles involved in serious personal Bible study for personal growth: teachability (receiving God's words), obedience (storing God's commandments), discipline (applying the heart), dependence (crying for knowledge), and perseverance (searching for hidden treasure).[23] Do not expect growth in assurance if you spend little time alone with God and do not take His Word seriously.

A former elder in my church who is now in glory called me one day just as I was leaving for a conference in California. He said, 'Pastor, I need to see you right away. I have lost all assurance. I am in dire straits – and in total darkness. God is angry with me. I'm thinking I must be a reprobate.' I told him that I would love to come over, but had to leave for the airport immediately, but that I would come and see him in two days. 'Meanwhile,' I said, 'spend thirty minutes with God each day – ten minutes in reading the Bible, ten minutes in meditation, and ten minutes in prayer.'

'I can't do that,' he said. 'My prayers would be an abomination to God,' he said. 'Do it anyway; not praying to God would be a double abomination,' I said firmly. 'Just follow my advice, no matter how much the devil tells you not to.'

When I returned home, there was a note on my chair: 'No need to see Elder N., all is well with his soul.' In his case, the solution was simple: get back into the Word, meditation, and prayer. The Holy Spirit used these ordinary means to restore his assurance.

---

23) Jerry Bridges, *The Practice of Godliness* (Colorado Springs: NavPress, 1983), 52.

If the Bible is to get into us and grow our assurance, we must get into it. Charles Spurgeon said, 'Backsliders begin with dusty Bibles and end with filthy garments.'[24] To neglect the Word is to neglect the Lord, but those who read Scripture 'as a love-letter sent to you from God', as Thomas Watson put it, will profit from it and grow in assurance. 'Think in every line you read that God is speaking to you', Watson went on to say; then, by the Spirit's enlightening, you will experience its warming, transforming, assuring power.[25]

Be consistent and disciplined in your reading of Scripture, remembering you are reading God's Word. Commit to a time, find a place, and develop a plan for reading your Bible. Approach your reading of Scripture with a reverential fear of God, being 'swift to hear, slow to speak' (James 1:19), determined like Mary to lay up God's Word in your heart. Approach Scripture with faith in Christ, looking on Him as the lion out of the tribe of Judah to whom it is given to open the book of God (Rev. 5:5-8; 6:1). Approach Scripture with a sincere desire to learn about God and about yourself. Come to Scripture with a teachable heart. Read for truth, wisdom, life, and love. Read the Bible diligently. Richard Greenham said that we ought to read our Bibles with more diligence than men dig for hidden treasure. Diligence makes rough places plain, the difficult easy, and the unsavory tasty.[26]

Study one Bible book, one chapter, one verse, and one subject or doctrine at a time. Ask yourself: What are these particular words and this particular verse saying to me in a practical way today? What is the practical truth I can apply to my own life here? Can I grow in my knowledge of a particular doctrine from this verse? Does the study of this verse prompt me to see some guidance for my daily life – perhaps something to be thankful for or some change that must

---

24) Blanchard, comp., *Complete Gathered Gold*, 62.

25) Cf. Thomas Watson, *Heaven Taken by Storm* (Morgan, Pa.: Soli Deo Gloria, 1994), 12–15.

26) Richard Greenham, *The Works of the Reverend and faithfull servant of Iesus Christ M. Richard Greenham* (London: Felix Kingston for Robert Dexter, 1599), 390–91.

be made, by the strength of the Spirit? Is there some sin exposed here that I must fight more earnestly, some righteousness that I must pursue more aggressively, some promise that I must embrace more fully? What should I experience from studying this verse? How should I feel concerning this passage? Should I respond with joy, sorrow, or a mixture of the two? How can I grow in assurance through assimilating my Scripture reading today into the very fabric of my life?

Meditating on what we read in the Bible is critical. You can read diligently, but the reading will bear no fruit if you don't stop to think about and study what you have read. Reading may give you some breadth of knowledge, but only meditation and study will give you depth and growing assurance. The difference between reading and meditation is like the difference between drifting and rowing toward a destination in a boat. If you only read, you will drift aimlessly; if you meditate and pray over what you read, you will have oars that will propel you to your destination.

Meditation can help augment assurance by preventing vain and sinful thoughts (Matt. 12:35), and by providing inner resources on which to draw (Ps. 77:10-12). Meditation serves as a weapon against temptation (Ps. 119:11, 15), provides relief in afflictions (Isa. 49:15-17), and glorifies God (Ps. 49:3).

Put into practice what you read by praying about what you are reading, by sharing with others what you are learning, and by pursuing holiness. As you read Scripture, develop a scriptural formula for obedient, holy living that can serve as a tool to assist you in your quest for assurance. Here is one possibility drawn from 1 Corinthians. When hesitant over a course of action, ask yourself:

- Does this glorify God? (1 Cor. 10:31)
- Is this consistent with the lordship of Christ? (1 Cor. 7:23)
- Is this consistent with biblical examples? (1 Cor. 11:1)
- Is this lawful and beneficial for me – spiritually, mentally, physically? (1 Cor. 6:9-12)
- Does this help others positively and not hurt others unnecessarily? (1 Cor. 8:13; 10:33)

- Does this bring me under any enslaving power?
  (1 Cor. 6:12)[27]

Read and study the Bible to be wise; believe it to be safe; practice it to be holy. Lay hold of it until it lays hold of you. Let Scripture be your compass to guide you in cultivating assurance and holiness, in making life's decisions, and in encountering the high waves of personal affliction.

The Sacraments

Use the sacraments of baptism and the Lord's Supper diligently as means of grace to strengthen your faith in Christ. Though the Word and the promises of God remain primary in assurance, the sacraments are divine seals that confirm God's eternal commitments to His elect, thereby enlarging assurance. Burgess wrote, 'Although God's promises to us will not be broken, and nothing can be surer than that, yet He adds sacraments to seal and confirm His promises to us.'[28] When the believer receives the sacraments by faith, he receives certification of that which is promised by God and renews covenant with Him. Covenant assurance and obligation then unite. The promises of God are made visible, cyclical, and personal in the sacraments.

God's sacraments complement His Word. They point us away from ourselves. Each sign – the water, the bread, the wine – directs us to believe in Christ and His sacrifice on the cross. The sacraments are visible means through which He invisibly communes with us and we with Him, by which He gives Himself to us and we receive and feed on Him by faith. The sacraments are spurs to Christlikeness and therefore to holiness and assurance.

The Puritans often spoke of 'sacramental assurance' – not because the assurance believers receive in the sacraments is different from that received under the preached Word, but because it was a common

---

27) I owe most of this formula to Sinclair Ferguson who gave it in a PhD class at Westminster Seminary in the early 1980s.

28) *Faith Seeking Assurance*, 145–6 (*Spiritual Refining*, 53).

experience of God's people to receive large dosages of assurance as they received the sacraments with faith, focusing on what their suffering Savior has done and is doing for them. Both preaching and the sacraments convey the same Christ. But as Robert Bruce put it, 'While we do not get a better Christ in the sacraments than we do in the Word, there are times when we get Christ better.'[29]

This begs the conscience question of some Christians: 'Should I abstain from partaking of the Lord's Supper when I struggle with low levels of assurance, or indeed, with whether I have any assurance at all? Is it right under such a condition to neglect the command of Christ to partake of the Lord's Supper in remembrance of Him?'

The tender consciences of Christians who lack assurance of faith ought to remember that the Lord's Supper is peculiarly designed to strengthen weak faith – hence it intends to be an 'assuring sacrament' in which Christ assures the weak believer that as surely as he, by true faith, eats and drinks the bread and wine in remembrance of Him, so surely he may be assured that all his sins are forgiven through Christ's sacrificial, substitutionary death. The *Heidelberg Catechism* (Q. 75) underscores this powerfully when it states:

> Christ has commanded me and *all* [emphasis added] believers to eat of this broken bread and to drink of this cup in remembrance of Him, adding these promises: first, that His body was offered and broken on the cross for me, and His blood shed for me, as certainly as I see with my eyes the bread of the Lord broken for me and the cup communicated to me; and further, that He feeds and nourishes my soul to everlasting life, with His crucified body and shed blood, as assuredly as I receive from the hands of the minister, and taste with my mouth the bread and cup of the Lord, as certain signs of the body and blood of Christ.

The *Westminster Larger Catechism* addresses this issue even more pointedly and pastorally:

> *Q. 172. May one who doubteth of his being in Christ, or of his due preparation, come to the Lord's Supper?*

---

29) Robert Bruce, *The Mystery of the Lord's Supper*, trans. and ed. Thomas F. Torrance (Richmond: John Knox Press, 1958), 82.

A. One who doubteth of his being in Christ, or of his due preparation to the sacrament of the Lord's Supper, may have true interest in Christ, though he be not yet assured thereof; and in God's account hath it, if he be duly affected with the apprehension of the want of it, and unfeignedly desires to be found in Christ, and to depart from iniquity: in which case (because promises are made, and this sacrament is appointed, for the relief even of weak and doubting Christians) he is to bewail his unbelief, and labor to have his doubts resolved; and, so doing, he may and ought to come to the Lord's supper, that he may be further strengthened.

Practically speaking, I also wish to add to these clear confessional statements that in pastoral experience of over four decades, I have repeatedly observed that when needy believers with low levels of assurance do come to the Lord's Table, their faith is commonly strengthened and their assurance grows, but when they abstain from partaking and neglect the command of Christ, they commonly bring a period of spiritual darkness over their own souls.

Prayer

Word and sacrament must be accompanied by prayer. 'We must give all diligence and heed to obtain this privilege [of assurance]', Burgess wrote. 'We must make it our business to importunately beg for assurance in prayer.'[30]

Take every phrase of John Bunyan's remarkably helpful definition of prayer and turn it into a petition that God would teach you to pray with assurance: 'Prayer is a sincere, sensible, affectionate pouring out of the heart or soul to God, through Christ, in the strength and assistance of the Holy Spirit, for such things as God has promised, according to his Word, for the good of the church, with submission in faith to the will of God.'[31] And then remember these two wise Bunyanesque applications of his own definition: 'You can do more than pray, after you have prayed, but you cannot do more than pray

---

30) *Faith Seeking Assurance*, 174–5 (*Spiritual Refining*, 673); cf. Burgess, *The True Doctrine of Iustification*, 273.

31) John Bunyan, *Prayer* (reprint, Edinburgh: Banner of Truth Trust, 2007), 1.

until you have prayed';[32] 'Pray often, for prayer is a shield to the soul, a sacrifice to God, and a scourge for Satan.'[33]

If you would grow in assurance, *take hold of yourself in prayer*: treasure the value of prayer, maintain the priority of prayer, speak with sincerity to God in prayer, cultivate a continual attitude and spirit of prayer, be an intercessory petitioner, and read the Bible for prayer. *Take hold of God in prayer*: bring God His own Word in prayer, plead His promises in prayer, lay hold of the blessed Trinity in each of His persons, and believe that God answers prayer.[34] By the Spirit's grace, through taking hold of both God and yourself in prayer, you will almost certainly experience, as Francis Taylor said, 'The more we seek God's favor by fervent prayer, the more will He assure us.'[35] And William Gouge added, 'Prayer is the most principal means of obtaining blessing, blessing from God.... That which through His grace He promises, upon the prayers of His saints, He performs.'[36]

Afflictions

Though afflictions cannot technically be called a means, God uses conflicts, doubts, and trials to mature the believer's faith. Assurance usually follows intense spiritual warfare; it wears battle scars. Burgess wrote, 'This privilege of assurance is given to those who have been acquainted with God for a long time, are much exercised in his ways, and have endured much for Him.'[37] Assurance is the fruit of strengthened and seasoned faith. Not that age and experience

---

32) I. D. E. Thomas, comp., *The Golden Treasury of Puritan Quotations* (Chicago: Moody Press, 1975), 210.

33) John Bunyan, *The Works of John Bunyan*, ed. George Offor (1854; reprint, Edinburgh: Banner of Truth Trust, 1991), 1:65.

34) For a more detailed explanation of these thoughts, see my chapter, 'Prayerful Praying Today', in *Taking Hold of God: Reformed and Puritan Perspectives on Prayer*, ed. Joel R. Beeke and Brian G. Najapfour (Grand Rapids: Reformation Heritage Books, 2011), 223–40.

35) Francis Taylor, *Gods Choise and Mans Diligence* (London, 1625), 199.

36) William Gouge, *The Right VVay* (London: A. Miller for Ioshua Kirton, 1648), 17–18.

37) *Faith Seeking Assurance*, 97 (*Spiritual Refining*, 35).

guarantee assurance, however, or that new converts cannot be blessed with assurance. As Burgess went on to say, 'That is not to say that God does not grant assurance at times to new converts who discover the love of His espousals to them because they are spiritually tender and need it, being much oppressed by sin. As Aristotle said, parents are often most tender to their youngest child because that child is least capable of caring for himself or herself.'[38]

If you truly want to grow in assurance, therefore, prayerfully use the ordinary means of Scripture, the sacraments, prayer, and even your afflictions, while walking with a good conscience before God. Couple these means with other valuable spiritual disciplines that we don't have time or space to cover in this short book, such as reading sound biblical literature, fellowshipping with believers, sanctifying the Lord's Day, keeping a spiritual journal, evangelizing, and serving others. God can bless each of these to help grow your assurance. As a general rule, assurance sought diligently through divine means of grace and the spiritual disciplines will be granted by God in varying degrees.[39]

The Duty of Pursuing Assurance

Next, *Westminster Confession* 18.3 says that 'it is the duty of every one to give all diligence to make his calling and election sure' (cf. 2 Pet. 1:10). Burgess affirmed the *Westminster Confession*'s conviction that assurance must be pursued as a duty.[40] As concerned souls, we should never rest until we can say that God is our God.

In a sermon on particular election Charles Spurgeon stressed that our duty to make our calling and election sure is not a duty we pursue 'towards God, for they are sure to Him: make them sure to yourself. Be quite certain of them; be fully satisfied about them.' Spurgeon went on to say that the way to go about this is to give '*all* diligence' to this task. God's ordinary way of bringing believers to

---

38) *Faith Seeking Assurance*, 97 (*Spiritual Refining*, 35).

39) Burgess, *The True Doctrine of Iustification*, 273.

40) *Faith Seeking Assurance*, 174–5 (*Spiritual Refining*, 673).

assurance of faith is not 'by some revelation, some dream, and some mystery', he added, but through diligent labor: 'Idle men have no right to assurance.... If thou wouldst get out of a doubting state, get out of an idle state; if thou wouldst get out of a trembling state, get out of an indifferent lukewarm state; for lukewarmness and doubting, and laziness and trembling, very naturally go hand in hand. If thou wouldst enjoy the eminent grace of the full assurance of faith under the blessed Spirit's influence and assistance, do what the Scripture tells thee – "Give diligence to make your calling and election sure."' Spurgeon then expounded Peter's list of divine graces in the preceding six verses, showing us how to achieve assurance, by the Spirit's grace. First, we receive God's 'exceeding great and precious promises', which are always the primary foundation of assurance (v. 4). Second, 'be diligent in your *faith*...hanging alone on Christ.... Give diligence next to thy *courage*. Labour to get *virtue*.... Study well the Scriptures and get *knowledge*.... Add to thy knowledge *temperance*.... And then add to it by God's Holy Spirit *patience*.... And when you have that, get *godliness*.... And then add to that brotherly kindness and "*charity*."[41]

In short, God commands us to pursue assurance prayerfully and fervently, promising that He will bless it. 'A good improvement of what we have of the grace of God at present, pleases God, and engages Him to give us more', Bunyan wrote. 'Therefore, get more grace.'[42]

William Guthrie explained succinctly how that works: 'Learn to lay your weight upon the blood of Christ, and study purity and holiness in all manner of conversation; and pray for the witness of God's Spirit to join with the blood and the water; and His testimony added unto those will establish you in the faith of an interest in Christ.'[43]

---

41) Charles Spurgeon, *Metropolitan Tabernacle*, 10 (1864):132–3.

42) Cited in Richard L. Greaves, *John Bunyan* (Grand Rapids: Eerdmans, 1969), 149.

43) Guthrie, *The Christian's Great Interest*, 196.

Thomas Brooks provided a helpful list of ways for you to pursue the duty of maintaining and strengthening your assurance: (1) be diligent in using the means of grace and spiritual disciplines through which you first gained assurance, such as prayer, reading and hearing the Word, the Lord's Supper, and the communion of saints; (2) meditate often on your spiritual and eternal privileges, such as your adoption, justification, and reconciliation; (3) value Christ even more than your assurance and your graces; (4) use the degree of assurance you have to strengthen your soul against temptations and corruptions, and to improve your Christian resolutions, affections, and life; (5) walk humbly with your God; and (6) guard against those sins that have damaged the assurance of other believers, and consider solemnly the dreadful evils that would accompany your loss of assurance – including the difficulties of reviving it.[44]

Moreover, this duty – when seriously engaged in – will assist us in other duties of the Christian life. The Puritan stress on duty reinforced the conviction that assurance must never be regarded as only the privilege of exceptional saints. The failure to believe that at least some degree of assurance is normative for the believer tends to leave us in a fruitless spiritual condition.

The Fruits Produced by Assurance

Finally, *Westminster* 18.3 stresses that assurance produces God-glorifying, delightful fruit, so that the believer's 'heart may be enlarged in peace and joy in the Holy Ghost, in love and thankfulness to God, and in strength and cheerfulness in the duties of obedience, the proper fruits of this assurance; so far is it from inclining men to looseness'.

Assurance elevates God-glorifying and soul-satisfying emotion. It produces holy living marked by spiritual peace, joyful love, humble gratitude, cheerful obedience, and heartfelt mortification of sin.[45] The triumphant and genuine love it produces for God and

---

44) Brooks, *Heaven on Earth*, 306–11.

45) Owen, *Of the Mortification of Sin*, in *Works*, 6:33–53.

for others forges fellowship, stimulates service, and energizes earnest evangelism. Thomas Brooks said,

> Genuine assurance will strongly put a man upon the winning of others; a soul under assurance is unwilling to go to heaven without company.... It will make every mercy sweet, every duty sweet, every ordinance sweet, and every providence sweet. It will rid you of all your sinful fears and cares. It will give you ease under every burden, and make death more desirable than life. It will make you more strong to resist temptation, more victorious over opposition, and more silent in every difficult condition. Genuine assurance will turn every winter night into a summer's day, every cross into a crown, and every wildness into a paradise. Genuine assurance will be a sword to defend you, a staff to support you, a cordial to strengthen you, a plaster to heal you, and a star to lead you.[46]

In a word, assurance enables faith to reach greater heights, from which all other aspects of Christian character flow. This invigoration of faith results in a new release of spiritual energy at every point in a person's Christian life. Thomas Goodwin called it a new edition of all of a Christian's graces that deepens his communion with the triune God and enlarges his prayer life – especially intercessory prayer.[47]

Burgess detailed the fruits of assurance even more broadly:

> First, assurance allows us to have excellent fellowship and acquaintance with God. The church that can say, 'I am my beloved's and my beloved is mine' (Song of Songs 6:3), abounds in spiritual community with Christ. In contrast to assurance, fears and doubts keep us aloof from Christ and make us slavishly tremble before Him.
>
> Second, assurance produces a filial and evangelical frame of heart. The spirit of adoption that enables us to call God our Father also gives us the humble disposition of sons, enables us to serve Him from pure intentions and motives.
>
> Third, assurance will support us even when we are experiencing nothing but outward misery and trouble. In those times when we

---

46) Brooks, *The Crown and Glory of Christianity, or Holiness, the Only Way to Happiness*, in *Works*, 4:235.

47) Goodwin, *Works*, 1:251.

cannot be assured of anything, such as our homes, safety, or lives, assurance of God's grace worked in our souls will be a wall of marble that cannot be beaten down....

Fourth, assurance of God's love will motivate us to pray. Prayer kindles desires, increases hope, and makes the soul more importunate....

Fifth, assurance makes a man walk with much tenderness against sin, for such evil would put him out of the heaven of experiencing how sweet the Lord is and how greatly His favor is to be prized. He will take heed that he does not rob himself of so great a treasure....

Sixth, assurance makes a man impatient and earnest for the return of Christ.... If the beginnings of assurance in this life are so wonderful and excellent, what will heaven itself be like, where all fears are abandoned!...

Seventh, [assurance provides] a full acquiescence to and resting in God and Christ [which] are sufficient to meet every need, so that they desire nothing in heaven but Christ and nothing on earth besides Him.[48]

Burgess expounded these wonderful advantages of possessing assurance of faith in his last sermon on the subject:

Assurance enflames and enlarges the soul to love God.... [It] breeds much spiritual strength and heavenly ability to perform all graces and duties in holiness with lively vigor.... [It] is a strong and mighty buckler against all the violent assaults and temptations that the devil uses against the godly.... [It] is a special means to bring contentment of mind, and a thankful, cheerful heart in every condition.... [It] is a sure and special antidote against death and all fears of it.[49]

Let me highlight four wonderful fruits of assurance in closing this chapter. First, *assurance transforms trials.* In the middle of Job's unspeakable trials, he famously confessed unspeakable assurance: 'For I know that my redeemer liveth, and that he shall stand at the latter day upon the earth: and though after my skin worms destroy this body, yet in my flesh shall I see God: whom I shall see for myself, and mine eyes shall behold, and not another; though my reins be consumed within

---

48) *Faith Seeking Assurance,* 69–71 (*Spiritual Refining,* 26).

49) *Faith Seeking Assurance,* 195–201 (*Spiritual Refining,* 681–3).

me' (Job 19:25-27). Notice all the personal pronouns Job uses here: *my* Redeemer, *my* flesh, *I* shall see, *mine* eyes shall behold. Assurance transforms him while in the middle of the sorest of trials.

There was a father who had a blind son named Johnny whom he took to the hospital for treatment. When the doctor entered the room, he rather coldly introduced himself, walked over to the father, took the child out of his arms, and walked away with him to do a test. The father quickly followed, saying with angst: 'Johnny, you don't know the doctor who is holding you; are you afraid?' Johnny replied, 'Father, I don't know the person, but I know that *you* know.' That is what the Christian feels in the middle of trials. We often don't know what is going on or why; we are encompassed with confusion and uncertainty. We have no answers, but we can say, 'I don't know, but I know my Father knows. I know my heavenly Father loves me and keeps me in His heart, His hand, and His eye – and that transforms everything.'

Second, *assurance produces contentment*. The hymn writer Fanny Crosby was converted as a young girl but she developed an awful flu, and the medicine in those days was very primitive. A doctor tragically prescribed a mustard poultice for her inflamed eyes, and the result was that it blinded her at the age of eight. She was taken to many doctors, including one of the best doctors in New York, who said she was going to be a poor, blind girl. When she heard that, she went home and wrote these words:

> *Oh, what a happy child I am*
> *Although I cannot see;*
> *I am resolved that in this world*
> *Contented I will be.*

Of course, this is the woman who wrote the verses, *Blessed assurance, Jesus is mine / O what a foretaste of glory divine.*

So this assurance brings contentment, even in the midst of sore and painful trials. We read, for example, in Habakkuk 3:17, 18, 'Although the fig tree shall not blossom, neither shall fruit be in the vines; the labour of the olive shall fail, and the fields shall yield no meat; the flock shall be cut off from the fold, and there shall be no herd in the stalls: yet I will rejoice in the LORD, I will joy in the God of my salvation.'

Assurance brings the contentment of being able to say: my heavenly Father knows what He is doing. He makes no mistakes, so I will trust Him. He does all for His glory and my good. Nothing shall separate me from His love (Rom. 8:38, 39).

Third, *assurance heightens holiness*. Assurance does not incline believers to 'looseness', the *Confession* says. In other words, it always distances itself from careless living and moral indifference. Far from making the believer proud, assurance keeps him humble, cheerful, and godly. It heightens holiness. Burgess wrote, 'By its very nature, assurance cannot breed arrogance or cause one to neglect God and godliness, [since it] is only maintained and kept up by humility and holy fear. When a man ceases to be humble or to have a holy fear of God, his certainty likewise ceases, even as a lamp goes out when the oil is taken away.'[50] The more a believer grows in gracious assurance, 'the more he grows out of himself', wrote Robert Harris, for then 'we become more humble and low in our own eyes'.[51]

Finally, *assurance hastens heaven*. Faith will get us from earth to heaven, but assurance brings heaven to earth. It gives us a foretaste of the heavenly experience. Thomas Brooks wrote, 'Genuine holiness will yield you a heaven hereafter; but genuine assurance will yield you a heaven here. He who has holiness and knows it, shall have two heavens – a heaven of joy comfort, peace, contentment, and assurance here – and a heaven of happiness and blessedness hereafter.'[52] And so assurance makes the believer long for heaven. He wishes in these moments of triumph and exaltation that heaven would hasten, that the days between earth and heaven would be shortened.

The apostle Paul had this heaven-hastening assurance in large measure. He says, 'I have fought a good fight, I have finished my course, I have kept the faith: henceforth there is laid up for me a

---

50) *Faith Seeking Assurance*, 192 (*Spiritual Refining*, 679–80).

51) Harris, *The Way to True Happinesse*, 2:91.

52) Brooks, 'A Cabinet of Choice Jewels', in *Works*, 3:502.

crown of righteousness, which the Lord, the righteous judge, shall give me at that day: and not to me only, but unto all them also that love his appearing' (2 Tim. 4:7, 8). He is, as it were, 'hastening heaven' here; he is saying, 'Bring it on, bring it forward. Let my corruptible body put on incorruption, and my mortality put on immortality. So I shall ever be with the Lord' (cf. 1 Cor. 15:53, 54).

In Romans 15:13, Paul says, 'Now the God of hope fill you with all joy and peace in believing, that ye may abound in hope, through the power of the Holy Ghost.' Assurance brings this new futuristic perspective to the Christian's life. It makes him long for heaven much more – to be far more heaven-focused on this earth.

In 1858, four hundred people died when the steamship *Austria* caught fire and sank in the Atlantic. Some survived, however, and one of them told the story of how several Christian men had done all that they could to get others into lifeboats before the boat sank. In front of them was the inky black, deadly ocean; behind them, the raging fire; under them, the swiftly rising waters. Five of these Christian men formed a circle to encourage each other about the joys of heaven. They joined hands, walked to the edge of the deck, and jumped into the ocean, with the expectation that they would arrive in heaven together. What assurance they possessed as they faced certain death in front and behind![53] Assurance hastens heaven.

Samuel Rutherford's last words on his deathbed were, 'Oh, that all my brethren did know what a Master I have served, and what peace I have this day! I shall sleep in Christ and when I awake I shall be satisfied with His likeness.'

May God grant to each of us who trust the Lord that wonderful assurance – more of it, longer spells of it – and may it transform our lives.[54]

---

53) Samuel Prime, *The Power of Prayer* (Edinburgh: Banner of Truth Trust, 1992), 160.

54) I am indebted for several thoughts in this last section to my colleague David Murray for an address he gave on the blessings of assurance.

❧ 9 ❧

Assurance Lost and Renewed

As faithful Puritan pastors, the Westminster divines concluded their historic chapter on assurance with a succinct but comprehensive paragraph (18.4) on how believers can both temporarily lose their assurance of faith and how they can renew and revive it:

> True believers may have the assurance of their salvation divers ways shaken, diminished, and intermitted; as, by negligence in preserving of it, by falling into some special sin which woundeth the conscience and grieveth the Spirit; by some sudden or vehement temptation, by God's withdrawing the light of His countenance, and suffering even such as fear Him to walk in darkness and have no light: yet are they never utterly destitute of that seed of God, and life of faith, that love of Christ and the brethren, that sincerity of heart, and conscience of duty, out of which, by the operation of the Spirit, this assurance may, in due time, be revived; and by the which, in the mean time, they are supported from utter despair.

The Causes of an 'Unreachable' Assurance

Causes in the Believer: Sin and Backsliding

This section of the *Westminster Confession* offers a magnificent link between Reformed theology and Puritan piety. It says that the reasons for a loss of assurance are found primarily in the believer. They include negligence in preserving assurance by exercise, falling into a special sin, and yielding to sudden temptation. Burgess wrote,

143

'It is true [that] the most tender and exact godly ones, as *Job* and *David* are ordinarily', experience like us that 'the more formal and careless we are in our approaches to God, the more are our doubts and fears'.[1]

Burgess said that assurance may be hindered, even lost, for several reasons: (1) Assurance can be diminished when we deeply feel the guilt of sin, for then we tend to look upon God as one who will take vengeance rather than forgive. (2) Satan hates assurance, and will do everything he can to keep doubts and fears alive within us. (3) Most commonly, the hypocrisy of our hearts and the carelessness of our living hinders assurance.[2]

Such causes are explained in the preceding chapter of the *Confession* on perseverance, which says: 'Nevertheless, [the saints] may, through the temptations of Satan and of the world, the prevalency of corruption remaining in them, and the neglect of the means of their preservation, fall into grievous sins; and, for a time, continue therein: whereby they incur God's displeasure, and grieve His Holy Spirit, come to be deprived of some measure of their graces and comforts, have their hearts hardened, and their consciences wounded; hurt and scandalize others, and bring temporal judgments upon themselves' (17.3).

That assurance can be weakened and diminished is also suggested in the chapter on saving faith: 'This faith is different in degrees, weak or strong; may be often and many ways assailed, and weakened, but gets the victory: growing up in many to the attainment of a full assurance, through Christ, who is both the author and finisher of our faith' (14.3).

First John 2:15, 16 warns us that those who love the world with all its lusts of the flesh, lusts of the eyes, and pride of life, will perish with the world unless they repent and return from backsliding. As common as it is dreadful, backsliding is a God-dishonoring, Christ-rejecting, Spirit-grieving, law-trampling, and gospel-abusing sin.

---

1) Burgess, *CXLV Expository Sermons*, 356.

2) *Faith Seeking Assurance*, 67–9 (*Spiritual Refining*, 25–6).

Backsliding is usually a gradual, drifting process unfolding over time. It often begins with the loss of interest and enjoyment in secret prayer. That in turn impacts a host of other decaying interests in the soul, including the private study and meditation of the Scriptures, the waning interest in the preached Word, the lack of fellowship with and love for fellow believers, slowness to confess Christ, the loss of evangelistic passion for the lost, and an inward coldness to all the spiritual disciplines. Increasing attraction to the world and the spirit of this age – its worldly entertainment venues, fashions, customs, places, and people – adds fizz to the soda of backsliding that does huge damage to spiritual health. Yielding to simple laziness (Hebrews 6:12 calls it slothfulness), promoting selfishness above service, failing to embrace God's fatherly and sovereign providences, tolerating unmortified sin that is not repented of, using entertainment that stains and hardens the heart, yielding to temptation and succumbing to patterns of disobedience, embracing man-centered hopes, denying Christ by abstaining from the Lord's Supper, replacing true self-examination with false presumption, allowing a double life that no longer earnestly fights against growing inner corruptions, flirting with and even engaging in secret sins long thought dead and buried – all of this and more cannot but impact the believer's assurance negatively.[3]

The *Westminster Confession* is clear: *The Christian cannot enjoy high levels of assurance while he persists in low levels of obedience.*[4] Then 'we chase away our assurance', Burgess explained. 'Nothing will darken your soul more than a dull, lazy, and negligent walk of life.'[5] For the Puritan, that was only right. If assurance remained high while

---

3) For an expanded treatment of the disastrous effects of backsliding, see my *Backsliding: Disease and Cure* (Sioux Center, Ia.: Netherlands Reformed Book and Publishing, 1982) and *Getting Back in the Race: The Cure for Backsliding* (Adelphi, Md.: Cruciform Press, 2011).

4) This is typically Reformed as well, as the German and Dutch family of Reformed standards make clear. Cf. Belgic Confession, art. 24; Heidelberg Catechism, Lord's Day 24; Canons of Dort, Fifth Head.

5) *Faith Seeking Assurance*, 175 (*Spiritual Refining*, 672–3).

obedience faltered, the believer might take for granted the great privilege of adopted sonship and grow spiritually lazy.[6] Knowing that backsliding diminishes assurance ought to keep the saints active in searching their souls. When assurance degenerates into presumption, it is good that doubts and fears prompt fresh desire for assurance. This urges repentance and acts of faith that may renew assurance. 'Fear to fall and assurance to stand are two sisters', wrote Thomas Fuller.[7]

The Puritan refusal to approve of assurance that coexists with disobedience refutes both Pelagian and antinomian tendencies.[8] It refutes Pelagianism, since the human will, stripped of divine grace, has no strength to reach or retain assurance. To the antinomian, 'unreachable' or 'losable' assurance implies that sin has serious consequences for the child of God. God's saints cannot sin without great cost. Sin grievously interrupts a close walk with the Lord (Isa. 59:2). 'Sin can never quite bereave a saint of his jewel, his grace, but it may steal away the key of the cabinet, his assurance', wrote William Jenkyn.[9]

John Owen compared unmortified sin that is not repented of to 'a thick cloud, that spreads itself over the face of the soul, and intercepts all the beams of God's love and favour. It takes away

---

6) Rogers, *The Doctrine of Faith*, 388.

7) Cited in *More Gathered Gold*, compiled by John Blanchard (Hertford-shire, England: Evangelical Press, 1986), 12–13.

8) According to Pelagius, there are three features in human action: power (*posse*), will (*velle*), and the realization (*esse*). The first is granted exclusively by God; the others belong to man. Cf. R. F. Evans, *Pelagius: Inquiries and Reappraisals* (London, 1968), and *Four Letters of Pelagius* (London, 1968). Semi-Pelagian tendencies later surfaced in Roman Catholicism, as well as in Arminianism's voluntaristic life of faith.

Antinomianism (*anti* [against], *nomos* [law]) teaches that it is not essential for Christians to use the Ten Commandments as a rule of conduct for daily living. The term was coined by Luther in his struggle with a former student, Johann Agricola. Agricola believed that repentance should not be prompted by the law but only by the preaching of the gospel through faith in Christ.

9) Cited in Blanchard, *Gathered Gold*, 8.

all sense of the privilege of our adoption; and if the soul begins to gather up thoughts of consolation, sin quickly scatters them.'[10] If you have allowed sin to dwell in your life unchecked, you know how terrible that cloud is of which Owen spoke. Consequently, Ferguson summarizes Owen's thinking by asserting, 'In the biblical teaching, mortification is an ever-present duty, because the presence of indwelling sin is a constant principle in men's lives.'[11] Thus, the basis of assurance cannot be sinless perfection; instead, Owen set up the hatred of sin as an evidence of faith (Job 42:6; Zech. 12:10; 2 Cor. 7:11).

Chapter 17 of the *Confession* thus offers a balanced view of perseverance: true believers can 'neither totally nor finally fall away from the state of grace, but shall certainly persevere therein to the end, and be eternally saved' (17.1). Nevertheless, sin will have serious consequences, such as (1) incurring God's displeasure, (2) grieving the Holy Spirit, (3) depriving the soul a measure of grace and comfort, (4) hardening the heart, (5) wounding the conscience, (6) hurting others, and (7) bringing temporal judgments (17.3).[12]

The conclusion is clear: Despite the great injury that ensues from backsliding, God's people shall persevere. Their perseverance is secured by their persevering God. Divine perseverance is Trinitarian in its outworking, consisting of the perseverance of the Father's eternal good pleasure toward them, the perseverance of Christ in His sufferings and intercession for them, and the perseverance of the Spirit working within them. Election, covenant, providence, satisfaction, and perseverance are inseparable from each other and from assurance. Thus, when the believer lacks assurance, the responsibility is primarily his. No enemy shall keep him out of

---

10) Owen, *Of the Mortification of Sin*, in *Works*, 6:23.

11) Sinclair B. Ferguson, *John Owen on the Christian Life* (Edinburgh: Banner of Truth Trust, 1987), 72.

12) Cf. *Canons of Dort*, Fifth Head, article 5a: 'By such enormous sins, however, they very highly offend God, incur a deadly guilt, grieve the Holy Spirit, interrupt the exercise of faith, very grievously wound their consciences, and sometimes lose the sense of God's favor, for a time.'

heaven, but he may well keep heaven out of his heart by sinning against God. Burgess concluded, 'It is therefore an unworthy thing to complain about the loss of God's favor and assurance if all your duties and performances are careless and withered.'[13]

Causes in God: Withdrawing and 'Tempting'

The *Confession* does not stop here. It also offers the possibility of God's involvement in the believer's lack of assurance. Unreachable or lost assurance may be the result of God's 'withdrawing of the light of His countenance' or of 'some sudden and vehement temptation'.

Does the *Westminster Confession* go beyond Scripture in saying that God has reasons to withhold assurance from some believers? Burgess said not. He acknowledged, however, that it seemed senseless at first sight for God to withhold assurance from a believer, for assurance is 'wings and legs in a man's service to God. It would enflame him more to promote God's glory'. Burgess went on to ask, 'How frequently doth God keep his own people in darkness?' He then offered five reasons God would withhold assurance from His people:

> First, that we may taste and see how bitter sin is.... Second, that God may keep us low and humble.... Third, that when we have assurance, we may esteem it more and take heed as to how we lose it.... Fourth, that we may demonstrate obedience to God and give Him greater honor.... Fifth, that we may offer comfort to others in distress.[14]

Thomas Brooks offered similar reasons for God's withdrawal of assurance, but added this important reason: 'That they [believers] may live clearly and fully upon Jesus Christ, that Jesus Christ may be seen to be all in all.' Brooks then went on to explain this rather surprising reason: 'Christians, you are always to remember, that though the enjoyment of assurance makes most for your consolation,

---

13) *Faith Seeking Assurance*, 95 (*Spiritual Refining*, 34–5).

14) *Faith Seeking Assurance*, 97–101 (*Spiritual Refining*, 35–6). See *The Works of Thomas Brooks*, 2:330–4, and *The Works of Thomas Goodwin*, 3:298–9, for similar lists. Cf. Rutherford, *Christ Dying and Drawing Sinners to Himselfe*, 49–50; *Influences of the Life of Grace*, 265; *The Covenant of Life Opened*, 219.

yet the living purely upon Christ in the absence of assurance, makes most for Christ's exaltation. He is happy that believes upon seeing, upon feeling, but thrice happy are those souls that believe when they do not see; that love when they do not know that they are beloved; and that in the want of all comfort and assurance, can live upon Christ as their only all.'[15]

We may be inclined to look askance at some of Burgess's and Brooks's reasons for the 'withdrawal of God'. But bear in mind two things: First, to understand Burgess and Brooks, we need to recognize that the Puritans believed that withdrawal on God's part was usually for holy reasons beyond the comprehension of the believer, who by faith simply must trust God's good intention. Second, those reasons were as so many pieces of a jigsaw puzzle, possible and partial explanations for that which a believer was experiencing. No Puritan offered a complete list of reasons for God withdrawing assurance. Rather, they grappled with the experiential and pastoral reality of times when they or their parishioners might *not* be backsliding, *yet* might lack assurance and feel distant from God. They were trying to deal compassionately with those who earnestly sought greater assurance but had not obtained it.

To understand this better, we should observe the connection between assurance and several doctrines taught in the *Confession*. These include God's eternal decree (ch. 3), His providence (ch. 5), and our sin (ch. 6). In the *Confession*, God's decree and providence extend to everything, including sin, desertion, and withdrawal. The *Confession* prompts these questions: May not God, who decrees everything for His glory, also get glory through withdrawing the light of His presence from His children in order to lead them in sanctified ways above their comprehension (3.3)? May not God who 'doth uphold, direct, dispose, and govern all creatures, actions, and things from the greatest even to the least, by His most wise and holy providence' (5.1) – a providence in which He is free to 'work without, above, and against [means], at his pleasure' (5.3) – also direct His

---

15) Brooks, *Heaven on Earth*, 38.

apparent withdrawals to their benefit? May not God who hates but forgives sin, chastise His children by withdrawing His felt presence in order to preserve within them a holy hatred for sin (6.5)?

In each chapter on decree, providence, and sin, the Westminster divines affirm a lofty, holy God, who rises above our understanding in complex reasons for being both a deserting God and a withholding God in the matter of assurance. God's holiness is paramount in this regard. The decree is described as the *holy* counsel of His own will (3.1). Sin is permitted in accord with God's *holy* counsel (6.1). Providence is denominated most wise and *holy* (5.1), and ordered in all things for *holy* ends (5.4). The climax of this holiness relative to God's withdrawal is in section 5.4:

> The most wise, righteous, and gracious God doth oftentimes leave, for a season, His own children to manifold temptations, and the corruption of their own hearts, to chastise them for their former sins, or to discover unto them the hidden strength of corruption and deceitfulness of their hearts, that they may be humbled; and, to raise them to a more close and constant dependence for their support upon Himself, and to make them more watchful against all future occasions of sin, and for sundry [different] other just and holy ends.

The key here is that *God is above us*. In desertion, in withdrawal, in vehement temptation, even in delayed assurance, God has His *holy* reasons. According to the Westminster divines, what God does now, we often do not know now, but shall know 'hereafter' (John 13:7) – perhaps tomorrow, perhaps not until eternity. But hereafter shall come. It is enough for us to know that God always carries Himself – both His 'comings and goings' – with twin goals in mind: His glory and the true benefit of His elect. Hence, as William Gurnall wrote, 'The Christian must trust in a withdrawing God.'[16]

In the matter of 'vehement temptations' (18.4), that is, sudden or extreme trials or afflictions from without, or internal trials or afflictions within the soul, the Westminster divines advised the

---

16) William Gurnall, *The Christian in Complete Armour* (reprint, Edinburgh: Banner of Truth Trust, 1974), 2:145.

following. First, when the afflicted believer receives no light for his soul, and the evidences of God's saving work in his life appear vague, he ought to cast himself upon God's promises, come what may.[17]

Second, even when God leaves believers 'to manifold temptations' (1 Pet. 1:6), He has His glory and their good in view. He will draw men to Himself and minister to them through affliction. William Twisse thus noted that afflictions can be 'as pangs of child birth, to deliver souls into the world of the sons of God'.[18]

Third, believers should appreciate rather than reject afflictions, for afflictions work medicinally to increase assurance. Afflictions wean the believer from this world, stimulate his spiritual growth, open new vistas of faith, increase his intimacy with God and submission to His attributes, and act overall as healing tonic for his soul. Still, Robert Harris said that this healing process may be so slow in coming that the believer may only realize it when he is healed: 'A man sees himself cured, but how and when [affliction] heals him, he sees not.'[19] But by means of the Spirit's sanctifying grace, the believer reaches heights of spiritual maturation and assurance that cannot be reached without affliction.

In sum, God's withdrawals and His placing of trials in the path of the believer are motivated by His *fatherly discipline*, which teaches 'right walking'; by His *fatherly sovereignty*, which teaches dependence; and by His *fatherly wisdom*, which teaches that He knows and does what is best for His own.[20] So don't despair, dear troubled believer. Soon, your heavenly Father's face shall shine in favor upon you again for only one astonishing and glorious reason: because His face was turned away from His own Son on the cross for the first time ever since eternity past; Christ was forsaken that we

---

17) *Faith Seeking Assurance*, 120 (*Spiritual Refining*, 43–4); cf. Sibbes, *Works*, 1:124.

18) Twisse, *The Riches of Gods Love Unto the Vessells of Mercy*, 287.

19) Robert Harris, *A Treatise of the New Covenant*, 1:44.

20) Rutherford, *The Trial and Triumph of Faith*, 326–9; Goodwin, *Works*, 3:231–6.

might be accepted of God and never forsaken by Him. For Christ's sake, God's face will shine on you and revive your assurance for His glory and your good.

The Revival of Assurance

According to the *Westminster Confession*, the difficulty of coming up to assurance does not negate the germ of faith in the Christian; the believer is never destitute of God's saving work despite his failure to see it. Indeed, the child of God may be losing assurance even while he advances in grace. As Rutherford wrote: 'Deserted souls not conscious of the reflex acts of believing and longing for Christ, think themselves apostates, when they are advancing in their way.'[21]

The *grace* and *essence* of faith abides with the believer even though he is blind to the *acts* and *practice* of faith. Faith cannot die, though its actions may wither to such a degree that the believer is unable to enjoy much assurance. As John Murray wrote:

> The germ of assurance is surely implicit in the salvation which the believer comes to possess by faith, it is implicit in the change that has been wrought in his state and condition. However weak may be the faith of a true believer, however severe may be his temptations, however perturbed his heart may be respecting his own condition, he is never, as regards consciousness, in the condition that preceded the exercise of faith. The consciousness of the believer differs by a whole diameter from that of the unbeliever. At the lowest ebb of faith and hope and love his consciousness never drops to the level of the unbeliever at its highest pitch of confidence and assurance.[22]

The essence of faith offers hope for the revival of assurance. The Holy Spirit does more than save the believer from utter despair in this condition; He does more than preserve the germs of faith and assurance within the believer. The Spirit's operations promise the revival of assurance 'in due time'. Though the confession urges

---

21) Rutherford, *The Trial and Triumph of Faith*, 139–40.

22) Murray, *Collected Writings*, 2:265.

regaining assurance by means of what Richard Sibbes called 'exact walking',[23] its final accent is on the irresistible operations of the Spirit.

As backsliding begins with the neglect of genuine prayer and dependency on the Spirit, revival of assurance begins with renewed prayer, confession and forsaking of sin, and a longing cry of the heart that the Holy Spirit not be taken from us (Ps. 51:11, 12), but return and resume His active work in the soul, as William Cowper describes:

O for a closer walk with God,
A calm and heavenly frame,
A light to shine upon the road
That leads me to the Lamb!

Where is the blessedness I knew,
When first I saw the Lord?
Where is the soul refreshing view
Of Jesus and His Word?

What peaceful hours I once enjoyed!
How sweet their memory still!
But they have left an aching void
The world can never fill.

Return, O holy Dove, return,
Sweet messenger of rest!
I hate the sins that made Thee mourn
And drove Thee from my breast.

The dearest idol I have known,
Whate'er that idol be
Help me to tear it from Thy throne,
And worship only Thee.

---

23) Sibbes, *Works*, 5:393; cited by Kendall, *Calvin and English Calvinism to 1649*, 109, 205.

So shall my walk be close with God,
Calm and serene my frame;
So purer light shall mark the road
That leads me to the Lamb.[24]

Assurance is revived the same way it was obtained the first time. Burgess maps out how this should be done. Believers should review their lives, confess their backsliding, and humbly cast themselves upon their covenant-keeping God and His gracious promises in Christ. They should use the means of grace diligently, pursue holiness, exercise tender watchfulness, and take heed of grieving or quenching the Spirit. In other words, they are to be converted afresh, which results in more assurance, godliness, and evangelistic zeal.[25] Only this return to the diligent use of the means of grace gets us working for God and yearning for His glory again. Such Spirit-worked conversion is a lifelong process of losing one's life and reviving assurance through nearness to Christ. 'Be always converting and always converted...more humble, more sensible of sin, more near to Christ Jesus; and then you who are sure may be more sure', said Thomas Shepard.[26] As Hawkes concludes:

> The work of assurance is a continuing exercise, a cycle, but an ascending cycle because it is God working to raise the believer up to himself.... By a helical process of trust, obedience, evaluation, and learning, God draws the believer from an initial approbation of the way of salvation in Christ to a full restful assurance that encompasses all aspects of the believer's life and consciousness.... This is the very hopeful message of the Puritans' doctrine of assurance. It is by no means the heavy burden

---

24) 'O For A Closer Walk with God' (http://www.hymntime.com/tch/htm/o/f/o/oforaclo.htm).

25) Burgess, *Spiritual Refining*, 34–5, 673–5; Joel R. Beeke, *A Tocha Dos Puritanos: Evangelização Bíblica* (Sao Paulo: Publicações Evangelicas Selecionadas, 1996), 42–68.

26) Thomas Shepard, *The Works of Thomas Shepard* (Ligonier, Pa.: Soli Deo Gloria, 1990), 2:632.

of self-justification or even self-assurance, but rather the light yoke of faith in the work of another.[27]

In sum, if you are a believer who has lost much or even all of your assurance, do not despair. Keep running the race set before you, laying aside sin, looking to Jesus, the author and finisher of your faith (Heb. 12:1, 2). He will send His Spirit to restore you. You may have lost your assurance, but you have not lost your sonship nor have you lost the Holy Spirit's commitment to continue working in you. Even your awareness of your loss is His work in you! And don't forget: you may have lost momentarily your temporal happiness, but you have not lost your eternal happiness. Your loss is recoverable; if Job and David recovered their loss of assurance, why shouldn't you (Job 19:25-7; 23:8, 9; Pss. 30:6, 7; 42:5-8; 51:12; 71:20, 21)? Above all, remember that your loss here is only for a short time; soon you will have perfect assurance and perfect enjoyment of God forever in the eternal Celestial City. 'Wait on the LORD: be of good courage, and he shall strengthen thine heart: wait, I say, on the LORD' (Ps. 27:14).[28]

Conclusion

All the *Westminster Confession*'s statements on assurance have the goal of leading the church to make her calling and election sure by finding everything necessary for time and eternity in the Spirit-applied grace of God in Jesus Christ. Its other goals include meeting God's children in their concrete, daily life, by explaining the Spirit's work, and motivating the believer to grow in grace. As such, chapter 18 of the *Confession* is highly successful. Thus, Robert L. Dabney could affirm in the late nineteenth century: 'The Calvinistic world has now generally settled down upon the doctrine of the Westminster Assembly, that assurance of hope is not of the essence of saving faith; so that many believers may be justified though they do not have

---

27) Hawkes, 'The Logic of Assurance in English Puritan Theology', 259–61.

28) Cf. Brooks, *Heaven on Earth*, 311–4.

the former: and may remain long without it; but yet an infallible assurance, founded on a comparison of their hearts and lives with Scripture, and the teaching and light of the Holy Ghost, through and in the Word, is the privilege, and should be the aim of every true believer.'[29]

---

29) Robert L. Dabney, *Systematic Theology* (Edinburgh: Banner of Truth Trust, 1985), 702.

❧ 10 ❧

The Spirit's Role in Assurance

Throughout this book, I have stressed the importance of the Holy Spirit's role in our personal assurance of faith. Without the Spirit, we will either be kept from having assurance when we should have it, or we will think we have it, when we have no right to it. Only through the Spirit's work can we be assured that we are true Christians.

Because we are weak and in constant need of divine assistance, the Holy Spirit works assurance in us on behalf of the Godhead. Romans 8:16 makes plain that this is the special work of the Holy Spirit when it says literally in Greek, '*Himself*, that is, the Spirit bears witness with our spirit that we are children of God.' The Greek sentence in verse 16 begins with the pronoun *Himself*, giving emphasis to this divine work of assurance that we are the children of God by the Spirit upon and with our human consciousness.

In this chapter, I want to look briefly at the Spirit's capability to do this great work of assurance, and second, more largely, at the Spirit's evidences of doing this work as expounded by Paul in Romans 8:12-17.

Evidences of the Ability of the Spirit in Relation to Assurance

As God, the Holy Spirit is able to do this work. In His wisdom, He knows precisely what we need to comfort, encourage, and assure us. His power overcomes every barrier raised against assurance. His energy never varies or fades, so that even in the most demanding times in life, the Spirit testifies of our adoption.

In the divine economy, particular responsibilities rest upon particular persons. It is not that there is no sharing in most of these areas but there is special responsibility and involvement by one divine person in particular. This is especially true of the Holy Spirit and assurance. As our Lord prepared His disciples for His death, resurrection, and ascension, He told them that the divine Comforter would come in His place: 'I will pray the Father, and he shall give you another Comforter, that he may abide with you for ever; even the Spirit of truth; whom the world cannot receive, because it seeth him not, neither knoweth him: but ye know him; for he dwelleth with you, and shall be in you. I will not leave you comfortless [or orphaned]: I will come to you' (John 14:16-18). The despair of the disciples after the resurrection vanished with the coming of the Spirit in His mighty, indwelling power. His presence assures believers through the darkest times that we are not left as orphans!

This peculiar work of the Spirit is evident in the way that He affirms sonship or adoption. Galatians 4:4-7 parallels and amplifies Romans 8:16: 'But when the fulness of the time was come, God sent forth his Son, made of a woman, made under the law, to redeem them that were under the law, that we might receive the adoption of sons' (vv. 4, 5). Here the work of redemption through Christ goes beyond the forensic language to the familial reality, 'the adoption of sons'. But how do we know that we are adopted by God? Galatians 4:6 goes on to say, 'Because ye are sons, God hath sent forth the Spirit of his Son into your hearts, crying, Abba, Father.' Do you see the direct connection? The Father does not want us to live in suspense about whether we are truly children of God. That reality is affirmed by the testimony of the Holy Spirit in our own hearts, so that He urges forth the cry, 'Abba! Father!'

Evidences of the Witness of the Spirit in Relation to Assurance

The entire paragraph of Romans 8:12-17 presents a tapestry explaining the assuring witness of the Spirit. Paul sets before us six major strands in this tapestry, all of which work together so that the Spirit witnesses with our spirit that we are the children of God.

First, the Spirit's work in developing a sense of 'ought-ness' within us (v. 12)

The Holy Spirit affects our desires or works in us a sense of holy 'ought-ness'. That ought-ness means, as Paul says in verse 12, that we feel indebted 'not to the flesh, to live after [or according to] the flesh'. Paul is saying, 'There is a certain revulsion for the things of the flesh that is highlighted and amplified by the conjoining work of the Spirit upon our spirits.' When the Spirit sheds His own light on this holy ought-ness to live in accord with the Spirit and a holy revulsion against sin, so that we understand that He has worked within us the marks of grace, such as loving righteousness and hating the works of the flesh – which entails hating all sin since all sin is after the flesh – we may know that we are children of God.[1]

That Spirit's work of witnessing 'ought-ness' within us includes many other positive things as well:

- He bears witness to our spirit and mind that the whole of the Bible is true and illuminates the Scriptures for us, so that we readily believe the entire Word of God is authoritative for our faith and practice.

- He makes clear for us how we are to live, so that we learn to love God's law and run to obey all His commandments and seek to overcome evil with good.

- He cures us of our spirit of self-dependence in a large measure by giving us clear sights of Christ in His beauty and fullness, showing us that He is our all-in-all, which in turn makes sin exceedingly sinful and odious.

- He works within us a tender and respectful love for each person of the Trinity, and gives us a burning passion

---

1) For further detail on this, see chapter 6 above.

for fellowship and a deeper experiential knowledge and enjoyment of each divine person.

- He moves us to long to be filled with the Spirit so that we yearn to surrender to Him complete control of our entire lives and long to please God in the pursuit of gospel holiness and service.

- He stirs our souls and affections so that our hearts burn within us, enabling us to know His witnessing work of imparting Christ-centered peace and Spirit-endowed quietness in our souls.

- He provides liberty in intercessory prayer for our fellow believers and moves us to love them and commune with them about God and His wonderful truth, thereby delivering us from solitary religion. We learn by His witnessing work that we can't be loners, for if we have God as our Father, Christ as our elder brother, and the Spirit as our sanctifier, we will also have the church as our mother and fellow believers as our brothers and sisters.

- He causes us to know experientially some foretaste of the blessedness of heaven, which Paul calls 'the firstfruits of the Spirit' – the beginnings of the full crop or perfection of glory (Rom. 8:23). He moves us to long to be in glory and shows us that we truly belong there, for where our Savior dwells is our real home.

Second, the Spirit's help in mortifying
the deeds of the body (v. 13)

The Spirit uses this ought-ness, this not living after the flesh, to lead us to mortify or put to death the deeds of the flesh. Paul goes on to say in verse 13, 'For if ye live after the flesh, ye shall die: but if ye through the Spirit do mortify the deeds of the body, ye shall live.' Paul does not hesitate to identify the child of God as one who 'through the Spirit' puts to death 'the deeds of the body'. John

Owen explained what Paul means by 'deeds of the body': '*The body*, then, here is taken for that corruption and depravity of our natures whereof the body, in a great part, is the seat and instrument, the very members of the body being made servants unto unrighteousness thereby.... It is indwelling sin, the corrupted flesh or lust, that is intended.'[2]

But why does Paul use such strong language as putting to death the deeds of the body? Again, Owen explained, 'To kill a man, or any other living thing, is to take away the principle of all his strength, vigour, and power, so that he cannot act or exert, or put forth any proper actions of his own; so it is in this case.'[3] The work of Christ in His death on the cross laid the deathblow to the deeds of the body, but that work is applied in degrees throughout our lives as those in union with Him. 'Be killing sin or it will be killing you', wrote Owen, and then added: 'The vigour, and power, and comfort of our spiritual life depends on the mortification of the deeds of the flesh.'[4] Chiefly involved in this work, therefore, is the Holy Spirit, for it is only 'by the Spirit', as He strengthens us and brings to our aid the graces God has provided, that we have any success in mortifying the deeds of the flesh. In that process, the Holy Spirit engages our conscious minds and breathes affirmation that we are children of God.

So it is 'through the Spirit', Paul tells us, that we recognize our mortification as a genuine work and thus confirm our sonship. Here is the difference between those ascetics and mystics that by sheer strength of will and punishment of their bodies live in isolation from everyone else to mortify the flesh, and the child of God that lives in the world but is not of the world. The Spirit comes to the believer's aid so that he might be salt and light in the world about him while not loving the world or the things in the world. The Spirit does this by (1) making us alert to sin, to patterns of disobedience, to areas

---

2) Owen, *Works*, 6:7.

3) Owen, *Works*, 6:8.

4) Owen, *Works*, 6:9.

lacking discipline, to enslaving attitudes, to creeping strangleholds of pride. He alerts and exposes these areas, which leads us to (2) grief over our sin. Our grief over our sin affects us so that sin becomes odious to us. We become burdened about our areas of disobedience. (3) Then the Holy Spirit takes us back to the gospel, applying the sin-killing work of Christ at the cross, showing us that we are free from the bondage of whatever sins beset us. (4) He enables us to fight the good fight of faith, to put on the whole armor of God to resist the onslaught of the adversary. (5) And then, by His strength co-laboring with our fighting, He enables us to put the sword through sin. As this happens, the Spirit bears witness with our spirits that we are children of God.

Third, the Spirit's leadership in living as a Christian (v. 14)
Continuing in this same vein of thought, Paul declares in verse 14, 'For as many as are led by the Spirit of God, *they* [emphatic in the Greek] are the sons of God.' This leading is an ongoing activity demonstrated by the present tense and passive voice verb. It is the same verb used in Galatians 5:18, 'But if ye be led of the Spirit, ye are not under the law.'

The Spirit's leading is one of the most important evidences of being a child of God. 'These words' of Romans 8:14, wrote B. B. Warfield, 'constitute the classical passage in the New Testament on the great subject of the leading of the Holy Spirit.'[5]

What does this phrase 'led by the Spirit of God' mean? Few subjects are so intimately related to the Christian life as 'the leading of the Spirit', and few have adequate conceptions of what that means. Some ignore the subject altogether because it's enshrouded in mystery whereas others speak of it lightly and glibly and always feel they are being led by the Spirit. Some think the very expression 'leading of the Spirit' smacks of fanaticism, whereas other dear children of God shy away from it and thus from their privileges as well.

---

5) Benjamin B. Warfield, *The Power of God unto Salvation* (Grand Rapids: Eerdmans, 1930), 151.

The leading of the Spirit refers to that office of the third person of the Trinity by which He guides all believers – not just peculiarly eminent saints – through the wilderness of this life to glory. This leading is not the Spirit's first work in the hearts and lives of sinners. His first task is to bring them to new life. Before He leads us, He must regenerate us; He must quicken us.

But the Holy Spirit does not leave the newborn believer there; He not only regenerates and quickens the sinner, but from that moment on directs and leads his life so that he will begin to and increasingly live in harmony with that new nature implanted in him. The Holy Spirit works in us, the apostle says, both to will and to do in accord with God's own pleasure (Phil. 2:13). Based on the Word of God, the Holy Spirit directs our actions by enlightening our understanding and guiding our inclinations to do what is pleasing to God. This work of leading is essential for the well-being of the life of faith; if you are not led by the Spirit, you cannot be a child of God.

The work of the Spirit in leading consists of *illuminating* and of *directing*. Both of these are necessary. We need the Spirit both to enlighten our minds to inform us of our duty as well as to enable us to walk in obedience to God's precepts. The metaphor of leading is taken from the blind and the weak. A blind man who cannot see needs someone to take him by the hand, to guide him, to lead him. A lame person cannot walk in the way, and he too needs someone to support him. Those two things are combined in this office of the Holy Spirit. He guides and supports God's people. He enlightens their minds but He also enables them to walk in the way that leads to heaven.

Eric Moerdyk explains this well:

Do you see the beauty of this work of the Holy Spirit? Do you see how when God gives you spiritual life, He activates you? When someone leads you by the hand, you still must move your feet and walk along. You are still responsible; you still must act. But you act following the leading of another! This is the leading of the Spirit. He does not force you to obey God, but comes with sweet power to lead you. And when you resist His leading, that is sin. That is like trying to drive your car with the emergency brake still activated. There is this inner resistance and unhappiness about where you are going, and a tug to slow you down and make you realize, something is wrong. I don't belong here, I should not do this. This is what it means to be led by the Spirit of God.[6]

The Holy Spirit leads and guides us in God's ways, always in concert with *His Word*. God's Word is the standard by which we must regulate our lives. As David says, 'Thy Word is a lamp unto my feet, and a light unto my path' (Ps. 119:105). The Bible is our map that we must consult on the road to heaven. This includes the Spirit's more direct influences upon our minds and hearts, all of which are also Bible-based. The Spirit will always work in harmony with His Word.

Based on God's Word, the Spirit sometimes speaks to His people in an intimate, direct way. If you are a believer, you know what I mean. Sometimes the Spirit influences your mind by *biblical applications* that restrain you from going into the ways of sin and encourage you to go in the ways of holiness. For example, when we are tempted to commit a sin, the Spirit will strive with us so that we feel that we must not yield to this temptation because it is dangerous for us and is dishonoring to God. The Spirit leads us to fight against our lusts.

When God's children are not backsliding, they are being led by the Spirit who is constantly forming Christ in us, as Paul expresses to the Galatians (Gal. 4:19). Through the application of His Word, the Holy Spirit directs us in the way of holiness. The Holy Spirit never leaves us stagnant but affirms our adoption as God's children even in the middle of the spiritual conflicts that arouse the graces He has implanted in our hearts. In the process of exercising those graces in the Christian walk, as the believer is led by the Holy Spirit in pursuit of conformity to Christ, the Spirit bears witness with our spirits that we are children of God.

---

6) Eric Moerdyk, sermon no. 41 on *Canons of Dort*, Fifth Head, art. 10 (part 5) – see sermonaudio.com.

Fourth, the Spirit's impartation of the sonship of adoption (v. 15)

In verse 15, we find the consciousness that we belong to the Lord by way of a contrast, as Paul speaks of having received something as opposed to what we have not received: 'ye have received the Spirit of adoption' and not 'the spirit of bondage', or slavery that leads 'again to fear'. Paul here helps us in understanding the precise character of the Spirit given to us in Christ. He is not the Spirit of bondage. He doesn't keep us in indefinite bondage to the law or lead us back to where we started out. There's a necessary connection between the Spirit given to us and the knowledge of our own sonship in Christ, since He is categorically the Spirit of adoption.

This Spirit of adoption, therefore, is not something additional or optional, but it is something essential to the well-being of the Christian life. The Christian life, when properly lived, is life in the Spirit – the Spirit of adoption – the Spirit that will not disown the sons of God. Nor does that Spirit want the sons of God to disown their own sonship!

I have only one son. I care a great deal about how I treat him because he is my son. I am more patient with him and persevere more with him than with other young men because he is my son!

The fact that we are sons of God, dear believers, determines the Father's attitude toward us and should determine our attitude toward the Father. A son is not dispensable. A son is not hired help who can be fired. A father can't and won't just send his son away. A son is not a dog eating crumbs under his table.

There is a new liberty in sonship that belongs to the Christian – a liberty that affects every area of life. Sonship is affirmed as the liberty that is exercised in worship, in prayer, in embracing God's promises, and in embracing God as a personal Father. Paul demonstrates this in the text, saying, 'whereby we cry, Abba, Father'. Michael Barrett explains the commonly misunderstood term *abba* well:

> The *ab* part of the word is the standard Semitic term meaning 'father';
> the *ba* part of the word reflects the Aramaic way of making a word

definite. In other words, *abba* does not just mean 'father'; it means *the father*.... It is not to be equated with the equally phonetically simple expressions 'dada' or 'daddy' that English-speaking children so easily utter as their first appellation of their earthly fathers. *Abba* is not a nickname; it is not a childish term of sentimentality or endearment. Rather, it is an honorific title that expresses the utmost reverence and respect due to any father – and infinitely more so when referring to the heavenly Father.... Although not a trivial term of endearment, *abba* does express the intimacy of the father-child relationship.[7]

In contemporary language, the believer who cries out 'Abba, Father' with great reverence is confessing, 'the Father is my Father'. The Greek word used for 'cry' (*krazomen*) expresses 'the fervent utterance of the devout believer', as Leon Morris put it.[8] The word *krazomen* emphasizes that such cries take place in great need, but also that such cries take place as the child of God recognizes his sonship in prayer, in worship, and in responding to the Father's promises. That recognition comes through the witness of the Spirit. In our urgent need while in the depths of our own darkness, the Spirit suddenly grants us at times the divine right and intimate privilege of crying to Him from the depths of our souls, 'Abba, Father!'

Often the witness of the Spirit comes to us almost serendipitously. My good friend Derek Thomas once told me that when he visited Jerusalem, he encountered a wonderful example of this between a young boy and his father who was dressed in the regalia of an orthodox Jew. Since the father was walking much faster than the boy, every few steps the boy would have to run to keep up with his father's fast pace. The boy finally collapsed, and cried out to his father in desperation, 'Abba, abba, abba, abba!' His father turned around, bent down, scooped him up, and carried him away on his shoulders. Dr Thomas told me that he never grasped the beautiful word 'abba' so well as at that moment. That's it; the God of creation,

---

7) Barrett, *Complete in Him*, 182–3.

8) Leon Morris, *The Epistle to the Romans* (Grand Rapids: Eerdmans, 1988), 315.

the God of the heavens and the earth, the God who is holy, the God of the thunder of Sinai, the God who will condemn sinners to hell, that God becomes my Father in Christ Jesus, through the Spirit of adoption, and receives me into His family so that when I cry out with utmost reverence, 'Abba, abba', in all my need, He stoops down, picks me up, embraces me, and carries me forward. This is the distinctive blessing of the New Covenant, that we as believers may call upon God in a profound sense – 'Abba, Father', by the Spirit.

Most commonly the Spirit's witness may be known and felt as we join Christ's corporate body in worship, focusing upon the Lord, and our hearts are lifted to recognize with fresh love that God is our Father through Christ the Lord. At such times, we feel the intense consciousness of sonship because of what Christ has done for us on the cross, so that we can rejoice that God is our Father. At other times, we may be engaging in private devotions, or fellowshipping with another believer, or simply driving down the road when the Spirit may so witness with our spirits that we are secure in the salvation of the triune God, that we may cry out with Thomas, 'My Lord, and my God', and with Paul, 'Abba, Father', with all the intimacy that these tender yet strong words imply. In that cry, the witness of the Spirit is prominent because that witness is inseparable from the child-Father relationship. Consequently, in such acts of private devotion or in familial communion – especially while worshiping in God's house, the Holy Spirit bears witness with our spirits that we are children of God.

But there is still more. The Spirit's witnessing of our sonship of adoption within our conscience, based on God's Word, brings us into a whole new way of life. When expounding Romans 8:15, C. E. B. Cranfield said, 'In this one brief expression we find the whole of what it means to live in accordance with the will and the law of God.'[9] Using abbreviated language here, Cranfield indicated that if we can call God our Father, and if we can cry out, 'Abba, Father',

---

9) C. E. B. Cranfield, *Romans, A Shorter Commentary* (Grand Rapids: Eerdmans, 1985), 189.

this means that behind us is the history of our now belonging to Christ, having been given another mind; a different attitude; a new set of standards, values, goals, and purposes in life.

A father once told me that a child he was adopting – who was already living with him – once said to him, 'If I am adopted, does that mean I can be unadopted?' This boy was soon issued a new birth certificate and could never be unadopted.

The same thing can be said about our relationship with God. If he has adopted us, if He has declared you to be His child, that is irreversible. Forever you will be His child. Think about that; revel in it, and find great joy and assurance in the reality of it.

Fifth, the Spirit's witnessing with our spirits that we are God's children (v. 16)

'The Spirit itself beareth witness with our spirit, that we are the children of God', verse 16 says. I can be brief here, as we have already discussed the Spirit's witnessing testimony at length in chapters 6 and 7. But I wish to continue the focus here on adoption and sonship as inseparable from assurance.

There is a repetition of phrases in Romans 8 referring to sonship or family relations for the Christian as part of God's family, which includes 'sons of God' (vv. 14, 19), 'children of God' (vv. 16, 21), 'heirs of God, and joint-heirs with Christ' (v. 17), and then the explanation of our predestination so as 'to be conformed to the image of his Son, that he might be the firstborn among many brethren' (v. 29). Thus the theme of adoption runs through this highpoint of the Epistle to the Romans. Being adopted as a child of God 'is the highest privilege that the gospel offers,' writes J. I. Packer, 'higher even than justification.'[10] Justification is primary because our need for forgiveness and right standing with God is present. But adoption steps higher since the forgiven are now part of the family! Paul moves from forensic language in justification to family love in

---

10) J. I. Packer, *Knowing God* (Downers Grove, Ill.: InterVarsity Press, 1973), 186–9.

adoption. Packer then expounds several important truths about our adoption and sonship:

- *The entire Christian life has to be understood in terms of it.*

- *Our adoption gives us the key to understanding the ministry of the Holy Spirit.*

- *Our adoption shows us the meaning and motives of 'gospel holiness',* [that is], Puritan shorthand for authentic Christian living, springing from love and gratitude to God, in contrast with the spurious 'legal holiness' that consisted merely of forms, routines and outward appearances, maintained from self-regarding motives.

- *Our adoption gives the clue we need to see our way through the problem of assurance.* That is, like the Reformers and Luther in particular, we learn to recognise the difference between what Tyndale called 'story faith' as opposed to true saving faith. 'Faith,' declared Luther, 'is a living deliberate confidence in the grace of God, so certain that for it one could die a thousand deaths, and such confidence... makes us joyous, intrepid, and cheerful towards God and all creation.'[11]

This personal realization of being adopted by our heavenly Father into His family changes our entire lives. Like Jesus, our entire goal in life now becomes doing our Father's will (John 5:30). We now strive to control our thoughts, words, and lives by the conviction that God is our Father and we are His children. When Romans 8 is set alongside 1 John 3, it becomes obvious that our glorious adoption greatly impacts our every relationship, including:

(1) *Our relationship with the triune God.* We now find our greatest love in God the Father and His Son, so that we share as God's adopted children in the very love with which the Father loves His Son (John 17:23). We now find our security in the fatherhood of God, knowing that He will mold and train us according to His

---

11) Packer, *Knowing God*, 190–203.

eternal plan for Christ's sake. We find our security in Immanuel's atonement in fulfilling His Father's will and dying for us as ungodly sinners. We find our security in the presence of the Holy Spirit within us, knowing that He will never forsake us.

I know I am entering a realm of mystery here that is better felt than told, but, especially when we are cast down and afflicted, weak and faint, and are in trouble and trial, the Holy Spirit makes His comforting presence known and grants us a gracious reviving so that we are lifted in spirit. When we feel deserted, He comes and moves us to fervent prayer; we feel contact with the Father and the Son by the Spirit, and our hearts open so that we with unspeakable liberty pour out our souls in prayer to the Almighty (cf. Rom. 8:23-8). By the Spirit's felt presence, we experience fresh visitation from on High, sweet fellowship and communion with the triune God, such that we know we are the adopted children of God.

The Holy Spirit is the one bringing us into that sweet fellowship. What a joy it is for a believer to know that this Spirit inhabits us, and moves us to embrace God as our Father, and the Son of God as our Elder Brother. Speaking of the Spirit, Jesus says in John 4:14: 'But the water that I shall give him shall be in him a well of water springing up into everlasting life.' Later Jesus says, 'Out of his belly [the inner man] shall flow rivers of living water.' And John adds, 'But this spake he of the Spirit' (John 7:38, 39). So the Spirit indwells the believer, and there are times when the believer, in his own conscience, may co-witness with the Spirit's witness that he actually feels and knows that indwelling. At such times, the triune God and His truth is embraced with assurance, so that the truths of the Bible become more real and alive and precious than anything in this life. Adoption greatly augments our relationship with the triune God for good.

(2) *Our view of affliction.* Inevitably, our relationship with God as Father involves discipline because our Father will not allow us to be less than what He intends us to be. It affects the way that we face adversity, suffering, and difficulties because, as children of God, Romans 8:28 does truly mean that God is causing all things to work together for our good as His children!

(3) *Our relationship to ourselves.* As 1 John 3:3 says, 'Every man that hath this hope [of adoption] in him purifieth himself, even as he is pure.' Every adopted child of God knows that holiness is an important part of God's purpose for happiness in God's family. Thus, every believer wants to purify himself daily, by using the spiritual disciplines to mortify and put off the old nature and to put on the new (Col. 3:8-17). And when he does so as a believer, he will discover that his increased assurance of adoption by God combined with personal holiness will deliver him from a burden of cares, fears, and doubts. He will feel like a new person. All the advantages of being assured of his adoption and salvation will accrue to him, for assurance 'produces heaven on earth, sweetens life's changes, keeps the heart from desiring the world, assists communion with God, preserves from backsliding, produces holy boldness, prepares a man for death, makes mercies taste like mercies, gives vigor in Christian service, and leads to the soul's enjoyment of Christ'.[12]

(4) *Our relationship with believers.* Being part of our Father's family affects our behavior so that we have a desire to live as sons and to be like our Elder Brother, Jesus Christ. As God's adopted children in Christ and by His Spirit, we learn to love our brothers and sisters in Christ in a way that human nature could not forge. We now see every true Christian friend as a gift of the Holy Spirit. We recognize in each other the saving ministry of the Spirit through the marks and fruits of grace, and the Spirit enables us through godly fellowship to strengthen each other in assurance. The Spirit uses believers to help other believers on the way to the Celestial City. As Paul comforted others with the comfort with which he was comforted by God (2 Cor. 1:4), so believers move others to greater assurance through the assurance with which they themselves have been assured by God. As adopted sons, we learn to view the details of our days through loving family eyes – the family of God, even to the point of being willing to lay down our lives for our brothers and sisters (1 John 3:14-18).

---

12) Brooks, *Heaven on Earth*, 129, 139–47.

(5) *Our relationship with the world.* First John 3:1b tells us that this relationship will be a troubled one: 'the world knoweth us not, because it knew him not'. On the one hand, we share with Jesus the unspeakable love of the Father, but on the other hand, we share with Jesus the hostility, estrangement, and even hatred of the world. We ought not to be surprised when the world despises us, for it despised – even crucified – our Elder Brother.

(6) *Our relationship with our future hope.* Sonship certainly affects our hope, because as children of God we are also declared to be 'heirs of God, and joint-heirs with Christ' (Rom. 8:17). 'When he shall appear, we shall be like him; for we shall see him as he is' (1 John 3:2). We have a glorious, sin-free future with our everlasting Father, our Elder Brother, and countless brothers and sisters, among an innumerable army of angels. Heaven, as Edwards said, will be a sin-free world of love.[13]

What a future God's adopted children have! At times, the Holy Spirit may give God's children assured and special foretastes of it – especially as they draw near to the Celestial City. Here is one example written by Edward Payson (1783–1827), an American Congregational preacher, who wrote to his sister from his deathbed:

> Were I to adopt the figurative language of Bunyan, I might date this letter from the land of Beulah of which I have been now for some weeks a happy inhabitant. The Celestial City of my deathbed is nearly full in my view. Its glories beam down upon me. Its breezes fan me. Its odors are wafted to me. Its sounds strike upon my ears. Its spirit is breathed into my heart. Nothing separates me now from heaven but the river of death which now appears as an insignificant little stream that may be crossed at a single step whenever God should give me permission to go home. The Son of Righteousness has gradually been drawing nearer and nearer, appearing larger and brighter as He approaches. And now He fills the whole hemisphere of my life, pouring forth a flood of glory in which I seem to float. A single heart

---

13) For a longer treatment of these changed relationships, see Joel R. Beeke, *The Epistles of John* (Darlington, U.K.: Evangelical Press, 2006), 124–9.

and a single tongue seem altogether inadequate to my needs. I want a whole heart for every separate emotion that flows through me, a whole tongue to express that emotion. Oh, my sister, my sister, could you but know what awaits the Christian! Could you but know what I now know, you would not refrain from rejoicing and leaping for joy at my departure.[14]

Who taught Payson this? Obviously, the Holy Spirit! As the Spirit opened this for Edward Payson, I don't have to tell you that his conscience co-witnessed with the Spirit he was a child of God on his way to glory.

Sixth, the Spirit's assurance connected with heirship and suffering (v. 17)

Finally, this amazing section stressing how the Spirit assures believers of salvation concludes by speaking about the child of God's heirship (v. 17a) and suffering (v. 17b) – both of which are signs of adoption. Those who are led and adopted by the Spirit are 'heirs; heirs of God, and joint-heirs with Christ'.

The greatest privilege of adoption is *heirship*. God's adopted children are all royal heirs apparent and co-heirs with Christ. 'Men may have many children yet but one is an heir', wrote Jeremiah Burroughs. 'But all the children of God are heirs.'[15] Hebrews 12:23 calls them 'the firstborn, which are written in heaven'.

An heir becomes the owner of all that belongs to another person when that person dies. An heir has the full legal right to ownership because of the will and testament made by the person giving the inheritance. Receiving an inheritance therefore is always a bittersweet thing. On the one hand, you are gifted with an inheritance. On the other hand, that inheritance only becomes yours because your loved one has died. You are left with the inheritance instead of with your loved one.

---

14) Edward Payson, *Memoir: Select Thoughts and Sermons of the late Rev. Edward Payson*, 3 vols. (Portland: Hyde, Lord & Duren, 1846), 1:406–7.

15) Burroughs, *The Saints' Happiness*, 192.

How astonishing Paul's statement is: the sons of God are heirs of God! The Father sent Jesus Christ as the God-man to the cross to purchase the legal right for the holy offended God to adopt sinners by faith in Jesus Christ and to make them heirs of Him who is the legal heir of all that God possesses – yes, of *all* things, Hebrews 1:2 says.

But you will then ask why you lack so much in this world, or why you face so many crises. The answer lies in the assuring Spirit conjoining your inheritance with your suffering, because suffering is part of the inheritance. God has appointed His children joint heirs with Christ. Christ came to this inheritance by suffering in this world, and therefore God uses suffering to prepare His sons for glory. That's why Romans 8:17 adds that we are 'joint-heirs with Christ; if so be that we suffer with him, that we may be also glorified together'. Sons receive the discipline of their fathers, do they not? God disciplines His children and heirs to make us partakers of His righteousness and holiness (Heb. 12:10, 11).

The consciousness of sonship even values suffering in identity with Jesus Christ, as Romans 8:17b says: 'if so be that we suffer with him, that we may be also glorified together'. Suffering is not viewed as an end in itself but points to a greater end of being glorified together with Christ. The Spirit makes us conscious that Christ is everything, so that even in suffering we identify with Him, knowing that we also are following His pattern: suffering before glory. And in that process, the Holy Spirit bears witness with our spirit that we are children of God.

But glory is coming – glory and kingship together with Christ, Paul says: 'that we may be also glorified together' (Rom. 8:17c). The Puritans make much of joint-heirship with Christ in terms of kingship. As co-heirs with Christ, believers share in Christ's kingship, and therefore partake of the kingdom of heaven as their inheritance. Believers are made kings to the Father in His spiritual kingdom in three respects, wrote Thomas Granger: '1. Because they are lords and conquerors of their enemies, sin, Satan, the world, death, and hell. 2. They are partakers of the kingdom of Christ and of salvation; for we have received of Christ grace for grace, and glory for glory. 3. They have interest, dominion, and sovereignty of all things by Christ.'[16] Herman Witsius stressed that this 'all things' includes the right of 'possession of the whole world', which was given to but lost by Adam (Gen. 1:28; 3:24), promised to Abraham (Rom. 4:13), and repurchased by Christ 'for himself and his brethren' (Ps. 8:6), so that now all things, both present and to come, are His people's.[17] Ultimately, believers are lords and possessors of all things, because they belong to Christ, who belongs to God (1 Cor. 3:21-3).[18]

Simply said, dear child of God, this means that your Father in heaven who owns every blade of grass in the world, all the cattle on a thousand hills, and all the galaxies in the universe, and has given it all into the hands of Jesus who died for you, makes you an heir and joint-heir with Christ of all things so that all things belong to you in Christ – who can comprehend that? As Eric Moerdyk says, 'Every log you sit on is God's couch. Every color you see was painted with God's paintbrush. It is your Father's world and one of the main reasons He made it was to make you a home to live in. He gave you senses so you could share His pleasure in His creation. In Jesus He has made you an heir of all this – and one day you will live and reign together with Him over all things, being made kings and priests unto our God! This is what it means to be an heir of God.'[19]

Nothing in this world can match the inheritance of believers. It knows no *corruption* (1 Pet. 1:4) – not 'by outward principles, as fire, violence, etc.; nor by inward principles, as sin and other taints which defile' (see 1 Pet. 1:18). It has no *succession*. The heavenly Father and His children always live out of the same inheritance, so believers'

---

16) Thomas Granger, *A Looking Glasse for Christians, Or, The Comfortable Doctrine of Adoption* (London, 1620), [26].

17) Herman Witsius, *Economy of the Covenants* (Grand Rapids: Reformation Heritage Books, 2017), 1:452–3.

18) Perkins, *Works*, 1:82, 369.

19) Eric Moerdyk, sermon no. 42 on *Canons of Dort*, Fifth Head, art. 10 (part 5) – see sermonaudio.com.

inheritance is as unchangeable as Christ's priesthood is (Heb. 7:24). It faces no *division*. Every heir enjoys the whole inheritance, since God is both 'infinite and indivisible'. 'God gives his all, not half, but his whole kingdom' (see Gen. 25:5; Rev. 21:7).[20]

Conclusion

Romans 8:12-17 makes clear that the witness of the Spirit is an important part of the believer's life and assurance. It is a gift from the Father to assure His children that we truly belong to Him. Let us not be content with trite methods for procuring assurance of salvation. Let us see that God has given us the Spirit of His Son, so that we might cry, 'Abba! Father!'

But what if my love for God is weak and faint, and I don't have freedom to call God my personal Father with assurance? Go to Him anyway. Go to Him as your Creator and Sustainer when you are plagued with an absence of the comfort that He's also your Father. Go to Him like the prodigal in humble ways, saying, 'Father, I have sinned against heaven, and in thy sight, and am no more worthy to be called thy son' (Luke 15:21). Go to Him as your want-to-be-Father, crying out, 'I believe, Lord; help my unbelief; I very much want to be Thy child, and for Thee to be my Father.' Above all, go to the Father in the name of the perfect Son of God. Use the Lord Jesus Christ. He loves to be taken advantage of by us at such times! If you can't come to God as your Father, go to Him as the God and Father of the only Savior there is, your Lord Jesus Christ. Let Him bring you into God's presence and introduce you to His Father. He encourages you to come by the Son to the Father when He says, 'Whatsoever ye shall ask in my name, that will I do, that the Father may be glorified in the Son' (John 14:13).

Let these thoughts help you to keep coming to God even when you feel doubts about your sonship. Don't leave the heavenly Father alone – keep coming to Him by and through His Son, waiting on Him, until you, too, can freely cry out, 'Abba, Father!'

---

20) Drake, *Puritan Sermons*, 5:334; cf. Owen, *Works*, 2:218-21, and Burroughs, *The Saints' Happiness*, 196.

❧ 11 ❧

Final Questions About Assurance

Before wrapping things up in the conclusion, I want to address five questions that people often have when they grapple with the doctrine of personal assurance of faith.

First, I cannot deny that I am a believer, but what should I do when I don't feel close to God and don't feel very assured that I am saved?

Be persuaded that God wants you to find assurance by resting in Christ by faith; He does not want you to be forever searching for assurance like a hamster on a hamster wheel. Here are eleven suggestions that may assist you:

First, pray to God that He will grant you the light of His Spirit and show you that you belong to God and are saved.

Second, read some of the promises of Scripture – *particularly* those, but not *only* those, that have been precious to you in the past – and rest your soul upon them. Remember that William Spurstowe said that God puts all His promises, as it were, like coins are put in a bag, brings the bag to you when you read the Bible, unties the strings and pours them out at your feet, saying, 'My child, take what you will!'[1]

---

1) Spurstowe, *The Wells of Salvation Opened*, 8.

Pray for faith to believe that all the promises in Scripture belong to you, including those promises that have not been made powerfully sweet in your past.

Third, as an outgrowth of these promises, flee to the basics of the gospel that Jesus Christ came to save sinners just like you, and all the precious truths that accompany the gospel. Meditate on these grand truths, such as the stability of God's eternal election, God's constant care over you, your union with Christ through His atonement, and Christ's continual and effectual intercession over you. And then rest in Christ by faith.

Fourth, in dependency on the Spirit, examine yourself by some basic inward evidences of grace, such as: Have I learned to mourn over sin? Do I know what it means to truly hunger and thirst after Christ's righteousness? If you cannot deny that these and other similar marks of grace are your portion, then conclude that you must be a child of God since neither the devil nor yourself can teach you to experience these things in truth; it must be the Holy Spirit working them in you.

Fifth, ask the Spirit to bear witness with your conscience through the Word that you are indeed a true believer.

Sixth, use the means of grace diligently, 'especially the Word, sacraments, and prayer' (*Westminster Larger Catechism*, Q. 154).

Seventh, resolve to turn from your ungodly unbelief, to flee all lusts of the eyes and of the flesh and all worldliness and known sin, and to run the race set before you by laying aside sin and looking to Jesus (Heb. 12:1, 2).

Eighth, remember that your real identity is found in Christ, by reckoning yourself dead to sin and alive to Him (Rom. 6:10).

Ninth, consider the solemnity of what the Puritans called 'the four last things': death, judgment, heaven, and hell. Live more for eternity than for time.

Tenth, be comforted by God's faithful track record to you for years and decades.

Finally, pray again that the Lord will bless all the above efforts to regain the stability of your personal assurance of salvation.

Second, what do you mean by growing in assurance through God's 'faithful track record' (no. 10 above)?

Let me explain how I use God's faithful track record in my own life. When I married my wonderful wife several decades ago, I was assured that she loved me. My assurance went beyond the marriage certificate that we both signed. But now, I am even more assured of her love. Why? Because she has repeatedly told me that she loves me and has repeatedly shown me love in thousands of ways over the decades. My assurance of her love has grown over the years in the context of a daily, living, loving relationship that exemplifies her faithful track record.

God's track record is far more perfect even than my wife's. It is now more than half a century since He stopped me and brought me to initial faith and repentance. For the last fifty years, God's track record through His Word and His actions in providence has increasingly assured me in ways too numerous to count that He loves me for no reason in me but simply because of His eternal faithfulness to me in Jesus Christ. I am absolutely convinced that He has made no mistakes in my life. Even though He has been pleased to appoint for me some very deep and painful afflictions in my life – afflictions in some cases of long duration – I know that I have needed every one of those afflictions. I can say of God, with full assurance, 'As for God, his way is perfect: the word of the LORD is tried: he is a buckler to all those that trust in him' (Ps. 18:30).

The *Heidelberg Catechism* resounds with this kind of assurance in responding to Question 26: 'The eternal Father of our Lord Jesus Christ...is for the sake of Christ His Son, my God and my Father; on whom I rely so entirely, that I have no doubt [I have assurance!] but He will provide me with all things necessary for soul and body; and further, that He will make whatever evils He sends upon me, in this valley of tears, turn out to my advantage; for He is able to do it, being Almighty God, and willing, being a faithful Father.'

Let us trust God more (Isa. 26:3, 4). Let us learn to grow our assurance by meditating on God's faithful track record to us, confessing with part of the catechism's 28th answer: 'We place our firm trust in our faithful God and Father, that nothing shall separate us from His love.'

Donald Macleod expresses this concept of the daily experience of God's assuring love well:

> Assurance normally comes in the context of a living, daily relationship. Unfortunately, a good deal of Christian discussion on assurance closely resembles the practice of going back to check if the Marriage Certificate is in correct form, forgetting that confidence between parents and children, husband and wife, and, above all, between the believer and his Saviour is a matter of a living, ongoing, daily relationship. The multiplicity of loving acts, tolerances and forgivenesses is what fosters and strengthens assurance. No real marriage needs to go back to the title deeds for assurance. In the same way, it is our daily experience of the goodness of God that fosters our sense of His love. We cry to Him and He answers. We bring our needs to Him and He supplies. Things we hardly dare dream of, God gives us. The things we have done, God overlooks. Sometimes, of course, it is so demoralising, so humbling, to find that God is so kind. Sometimes in our perverseness, we wish that God would not be so loving. Then we could stand up and argue with Him and get some of our ego back. But no! The constant flow of acts of goodness and mercy fuels the assurance. There is nothing particularly mystical or dramatic about it, any more than family life is mystical or dramatic. But it is there: God listening to us, God hearing us, God answering us, God supplying our needs, not in some [stingy] way but according to His own riches in glory by Christ Jesus.
>
> Let's not be going back constantly to the Marriage Certificate (or the Birth Certificate) to see if God really loves us. Let's look, instead, at the way He treats us.[2]

What about you? Can you look back over your life and say, 'God has made no mistakes with me. Every day He has shown me His assuring faithfulness, so that I can say with Paul in the context of my relationship with Him that I "know that all things work together

---

2) Donald Macleod, *A Faith to Live By* (Ross-shire, Scotland: Christian Focus, 2002), 155–6.

for good to them that love God" (Rom. 8:28) – and by God's grace, I know that I love God.'

Third, how can I possess assurance when I still so often doubt?

Calvin said that it is ordinary for believers – even assured believers such as Abraham (Gen. 15:8), David (Ps. 31:22), and Jeremiah (Lam. 3:2-10, 18) – to have doubts at times. Doubt seeks to dislodge faith in nearly every pilgrim traveling to the Celestial City at one time or another. Yet, as William Gouge pointed out, the presence of doubt does not mean that faith is absent, as David and other psalmists make abundantly clear in the Psalms. When we believers doubt the reality of our faith, we must remember that our doubt does not arise out of faith but out of our human flesh's weakness, which will remain so long as we are alive (Rom. 7:14-25) – hence the cry, 'Lord, I believe; help thou mine unbelief' (Mark 9:24).

God never recommends or praises doubt, for doubt is unbelief, and unbelief is always sinful and the root cause of all sin. Though God's patience with doubters is staggering, He rebukes their doubts (Luke 24:38, 39), for doubt robs Him of His glory and makes Christianity look weak and ineffective to a watching world. Doubting is dangerous because it tends to put our feelings ahead of our faith; it contradicts the biblical teaching of putting right thinking and believing first, so that right living may follow. J. D. Greear stresses, 'Don't feel your way into your beliefs; believe your way into your feelings.'[3] Doubting is also dangerous because it 'distracts us from serving Jesus wholeheartedly', denies us 'answers to our prayers', robs us of 'the joy of our salvation', and challenges our bedrock belief that 'salvation is by faith'.[4] Doubt wars against our faith. Just as we must strive to subdue our flesh, so we must strive

---

3) J. D. Greear, *Stop Asking Jesus Into Your Heart: How to Know for Sure You are Saved* (Nashville: B&H, 2013), 108.

4) John Stevens, *How can I be sure? And other questions about doubt, assurance and the Bible* (Croydon, U.K.: The Good Book Co., 2014), 24–30.

to banish doubt lest it damage our faith, for, as Gouge concluded, faith and doubt 'stand together as two implacable and irreconcilable enemies. The combat must cost one of their lives.'[5]

Doubt is a hidden struggle many Christians encounter (Matt. 16:22; James 1:6). One reason believers are prone to doubt is because their faith is so small and unbelief is so strong (Mark 9:24). We're prone to forget that weak and small faith that is true is still genuine, saving faith. Eric Moerdyk says, 'Do you go to your garden and notice the bean plants just poking through the soil and conclude that just because you can't pick beans from them today, they must not be real bean plants after all? Why do you do this then spiritually to your own soul? The marks of grace that you can see are about spiritual works of God that only He can produce. When these evidences even begin to show themselves in your heart, they are proof of the Holy Spirit's work. Don't accuse yourself bitterly before God because you don't have as much of the Spirit's gifts and graces as you would like or as you should. But thank Him first of all that they are there at all.'[6]

There are many more reasons why believers doubt. Some of them are physical: their natural temperament, depression resulting from the cascading of trials, tiredness and exhaustion, and the oppressing burden of serious and painful diseases. Some of the reasons are intellectual. We try to reconcile clashes between the Bible and history, concerning such things as the inspiration and infallibility of the Scriptures. We may doubt because of conflicts between the Bible and modern science, concerning such things as the earth's origins and the creation-evolution debate. Sometimes we grapple with making sense of the Bible and suffering, such as the suffering that is taking place at any given moment around the world. And sometimes we doubt when we try to reconcile the Bible with huge philosophical and theological questions reaching beyond the boundaries of Scripture in an effort to solve riddles that are too big

---

5) William Gouge, *Whole Armour of God* (London: John Beale, 1619), 237.

6) Eric Moerdyk, sermon no. 39 on *Canons of Dort*, Fifth Head, art. 10 (part 2) – see sermonaudio.com.

for us – riddles whose answers are tucked away in God's secret will and are not meant for us to grasp and explain (Deut. 29:29) – such as 'whence evil', how we can merge God's sovereignty with man's responsibility, how we can understand Christ's two natures in one person, or how three divine persons can coexist in the one God. But most of the reasons believers doubt are spiritual: the ongoing burdens of original sin and the remaining power of indwelling sin, the lack of strong exercises of faith and feelings of love for God, the frustrations of seeing negligible fruits of grace in personal life and in ministry outreach, the enticements of a hostile world, the mysterious withdrawal of God's favorable presence, and the attacks of Satan who is the father of doubts. Satan is always trying to get us to doubt the infinite love, power, and wisdom of Christ, and our old nature is far too quick to credit his testimony.

Here are two remedies for your doubting: First, address your doubts before they injure your faith irreparably. Recognize the dangers of doubt just mentioned; confess to God and one or two of your closest, wisest, and most confidential Christian friends that you are struggling with certain things, and seek wise counsel from them, the Scriptures, biblical literature, and other spiritual disciplines to overcome your doubts. Don't let your doubts fester; confess with the psalmist to yourself that your soul is downcast and then counsel your own soul to hope in God: 'Why art thou cast down, O my soul? And why art thou disquieted within me? Hope thou in God: for I shall yet praise him, who is the health of my countenance, and my God' (Ps. 42:11; cf. 43:5). The Puritans called this holding soliloquy with your own soul – that is, in addition to reaching out to other persons and sources to counsel you in your unique situation, you become the counselor of your own soul, telling your soul, based on God's Word, what to do.

Second, let your triune God's work overshadow Satan's work. Here are some helps for how to do so:

- Trust in Jesus's great high priestly work, for He is 'touched with the feeling of our infirmities; [was] in all points tempted like as we are, yet without sin' (Heb. 4:15). Your sympathetic High Priest is almighty to deliver you from the spiritual bondage of doubt and doubting. As John Stevens writes, 'You have been clothed in His perfect righteousness, which He obtained by living a life of complete obedience and faith. He never fell into the sin of unbelief so all your doubts are covered by His perfect faith, which is counted as yours.'[7]

- Ask the Spirit for grace to obey Jesus's word to Thomas: 'Be not faithless, but believing' (John 20:27)! He is, after all, the Spirit of faith, grace, and supplication (Zech. 12:10). Ask Him for grace to truly believe in and rest your weary soul upon the precious doctrine of justification by faith alone.

- Entrust yourself to the Father and His promises, for the Father of all comforts is more powerful than the Satan of all doubts. One word of infinite love from His Word – such as Romans 8:28, 'We know that all things work together for good to them that love God, to them who are the called according to His purpose' – is able to bury a million satanic words and devices. Praise the triune God for that and go on trusting Him and His Word, without doubting.

- Maintain a close personal walk with God. That involves several important matters: Search God's Word daily, finding delight in both His gospel and His law. Memorize the Word, meditate on it, sing it, love it, and live it (cf. Ps. 119). Belong to a supportive church family; feed on Bible-based, God-glorifying, Christ-centered sermons (Heb. 10:22-25); and love the church as Christ's bride. Fellowship especially with the most godly people you know, remembering as Thomas Watson said, 'Association begets assimilation.'[8] Keep up a steady diet of reading sound biblical literature that can feed your soul richly.

---

7) Stevens, *How can I be sure?*, 61.

8) Thomas Watson, *A Body of Divinity* (London: Banner of Truth Trust, 1960), 87.

To that end, I strongly recommend reading the Puritans. They will draw you to God, convict you, challenge you, enlighten you, and comfort you like no other group of writers in church history can do. Keep a close watch on God's hand of providence. Let His past work in your life and in the lives of others greatly encourage you (cf. Ps. 78:1-8). Allow suffering to produce maturity in your life by bowing under your sovereign Lord's will (Heb. 12:5-14). Put your faith into practice through self-denial, mortifying sin, cross-bearing, hospitality, and evangelism. As you increasingly forget yourself and increasingly minister to the needs of others for God's glory, you might be surprised at how much you grow in assurance![9]

If, however, after following the advice above and throughout this book, you find that your doubts only grow worse and become chronic and unrelenting, I would advise you to seek pastoral help from a wise, biblical pastor. I pray that God will bless good spiritual counseling to your soul's relief, liberty, and assurance.

In sum, look beyond your doubts and trials, as enabled, to your assuring triune God. Though circumstances may fail you, your God will not. If He didn't fail Abraham, Job, David, and Peter in all their trials, why should He fail you? Though He promises hell to Satan, the father of doubts, and all his minions, to you who believe in His Son, He promises grace to the struggling here on earth and glory to the victorious in the Celestial City.[10]

Fourth, is faith a condition of the covenant of grace?

The Puritan writers said assurance is based on the covenant of grace and the saving work of Christ. In turn, the covenant and redemption are grounded in God's sovereign good pleasure and love in eternal

---

9) Cf. Stevens, *How can I be sure?*, 77–88.

10) For books that address the subject of doubting, see Obadiah Sedgwick, *The Doubting Believer* (Morgan, Pa.: Soli Deo Gloria, 1993); Lynn Anderson, *If I Really Believe, Why Do I Have These Doubts?* (West Monroe, Louisiana: Howard Publishing, 2000).

election.[11] Assurance flows out of the certainty that God will not disinherit His adopted children. His covenant cannot be broken, for it is fixed in His eternal decrees and promises. God's covenant may be viewed as conditional upon faith, but also as unconditional by sovereign grace.

On the one hand, the Puritans sometimes emphasized faith as a condition of the covenant. They cite God's promise 'that whosoever believeth in him should not perish, but have everlasting life', and 'He that believeth on the Son hath everlasting life' (John 3:16, 36). Hence faith is the condition of the covenant, and assurance depends upon the reality of faith. Ames wrote, 'He that doth rightly understand the promise of the covenant cannot be sure of his salvation, unless he perceives in himself true faith and repentance.'[12]

On the other hand, the Puritans sometimes emphasized the unconditional nature of the covenant. This is not a contradiction, for in the covenant God promises to give the conditions of the covenant. He says, 'A new heart also will I give you, and a new spirit will I put within you: and I will take away the stony heart out of your flesh, and I will give you an heart of flesh' (Ezek. 36:26).

William Bridge (1600–1671) quipped: 'What if the condition of one promise be the thing promised in another promise?... Now so it is that the condition of one is the thing promised in another promise. For example: in one promise, repentance is the condition of the promise (2 Chron. 6:37, 38; Joel 2:15-19). But in another promise, repentance is the thing promised (Ezek. 36:6).... The Lord Jesus Christ hath performed the condition of the promise for you better than you can perform it.'[13]

---

11) Jeremiah Burroughs, *An Exposition of the Prophecy of Hosea* (reprint, Morgan, Pa.: Soli Deo Gloria, 1988), 590. Cf. Peter Lake, *Moderate Puritans and the Elizabethan Church* (Cambridge: University of Cambridge Press, 1982), 99–104.

12) Cited in John von Rohr, 'Covenant and Assurance in Early English Puritanism', *Church History* 34, no. 2 (1965):197.

13) William Bridge, *The Works of William Bridge* (1649; Morgan, Pa.: Soli Deo Gloria, 1989), 2:132–3.

The conditional yet unconditional nature of the covenant lends itself to different emphases throughout Puritan teaching on assurance. John von Rohr pointed out that the Puritan teaching on the ultimate security of the covenant rests in the one-sided action of God's sovereign grace. Von Rohr explained:

> The Covenant of Grace is both conditional and absolute. Faith is required as a condition antecedent to salvation, but that very faith is already granted as a gift of election. As Ames put it, 'the condition of the Covenant is also promised in the Covenant.' For Ames, the promise of the fulfillment of covenant conditions is itself a covenant promise. Preston designated this as a 'double covenant' in which 'God doth not only promise for his part, but makes a covenant to enable us to perform the conditions on our part.'
>
> In the Covenant, in this final sense, grace does all, and reliance must be upon this promise…. The doctrines of total depravity and of total divine sovereignty could not be relinquished. Thus as God's Covenant was also his divine gift of faith to his elect, assurance must likewise look to the absolute character of his promises and to that immutable good pleasure of his will upon which all things depend.[14]

The Puritans taught that election and covenant reinforce each other. William Stoever noted, 'Puritan covenant theology offered troubled saints a double source of assurance. It allowed them to plead the covenant with God, importuning him to fulfill his part of the bargain by performing what he had promised; and it encouraged them to seek comfort in the sufficiency of prevenient grace and in the immutability of God's will in election, which underlay the covenant itself and their own participation in it.'[15]

God's absolute promises in election and the covenant convince the believer that even if he lacks the acts of faith at a given moment,

---

14) Von Rohr, 'Covenant and Assurance in Early English Puritanism', 199–202.

15) William Stoever, *'A Faire and Easie Way to Heaven': Covenant Theology and Antinomianism in Early Massachusetts* (Middleton, Conn.: Wesleyan University Press, c. 1978), 147–8. Cf. David C. Lachman, *The Marrow Controversy, 1718–1723* (Edinburgh: Rutherford House, 1988), 53–4.

he cannot utterly lose the principle of faith, for faith is rooted in the electing, covenantal God.[16] Not even sin can break that covenant.[17] Nevertheless, assurance is affected by the conditional dimension of the covenant. Peter Bulkeley (1583–1659) said, 'The absolute promises are laid before us as the foundation of our salvation…and the conditional as the foundation of our assurance.'[18] The conditional promises are inseparable from the believer's daily renewal of the covenant by means of prayer, meditation, worship, and the sacraments.[19] 'To gather up assurance from the conditions of the covenant is the highest pitch of Christianity', Thomas Blake (c. 1597–1657) said.[20]

Ultimately, however, even a believer at the 'highest pitch' must return to God's absolute promises, for, as William Perkins (1558–1602) said, 'the anchor of hope must be fixed in that truth and stability of the immutable good pleasure of God'.[21] This 'good pleasure' is not arbitrary, but testifies of God's faithfulness to His covenant. The God of election, of the covenant, and of absolute promises also grants grace to perform the conditional promises. So von Rohr concluded: 'Though grounds for assurance are in the conditional covenant, they are not removed from the covenant as absolute. Reliance must somehow be upon the promises of the latter in order that it may also be on the conditions of the former.'[22]

---

16) Peter Bulkeley, *The Gospel-Covenant; or the Covenant of Grace Opened*, 2nd ed. (London: Matthew Simmons, 1651), 276.

17) Richard Sibbes, *The Complete Works of Richard Sibbes*, ed. with memoir by A. B. Grosart (Edinburgh: James Nichol, 1862), 1:220.

18) Bulkeley, *The Gospel-Covenant; or the Covenant of Grace Opened*, 323–4.

19) John von Rohr, *The Covenant of Grace in Puritan Thought* (Atlanta: Scholars Press, 1986), 186. See E. Brooks Holifield, *The Covenant Sealed: The Development of Puritan Sacramental Theology in Old and New England, 1570–1720* (New Haven: Yale University Press, 1974), 38–61 for how the Puritans viewed the sacraments as fostering assurance.

20) Thomas Blake, *Vindiciae Foederis, or a Treatise of the Covenant of God entered with man-kinde, in the several Kindes and Degrees of it* (London: A. Roper, 1653), 5.

21) Perkins, *Works*, 1:114.

22) Von Rohr, *The Covenant of Grace in Puritan Thought*, 190.

Finally, how do perseverance and assurance interrelate?

We have observed that it is one thing to become a Christian, and another to persevere in being a Christian and be assured that you are a true believer. We are all at least vaguely aware that you can't have continued assurance of faith in the Christian life if you fail to persevere in faith. We sense intuitively that assurance and perseverance are not quite the same yet cannot be divorced from each other. So, how do assurance and perseverance assist each other in the Christian life?

First, let's define our terms. We've already seen that assurance of faith is the conviction that by God's grace, one belongs to Christ, has received full pardon for all sins, and will inherit eternal life. One who has true assurance not only believes in Christ for salvation but also knows that he believes.

As for perseverance of the saints, we first must ask, who are the saints? Many would extend 'eternal security' to all baptized persons, or to all who have made decisions for Christ at evangelistic meetings. Scripture and the Reformed Confessions speak only of the perseverance of *saints*, defined as those 'whom God calls, according to his purpose, to the communion of his Son, our Lord Jesus Christ, and regenerates by the Holy Spirit' (*Canons of Dort*, Fifth Head, Art. 1); and 'they whom God hath accepted in his Beloved, effectually called and sanctified by his Spirit' (*Westminster Confession of Faith*, 17.1). By the preserving work of the triune God (1 Cor. 1:8, 9), such persons will persevere in true faith, and in the works that proceed from faith, so long as they continue in the world.

Some theologians want to speak of the *preservation* of the saints, rather than *perseverance*. These two notions are closely related, but not the same. The preserving activity of God undergirds the saints' perseverance. He keeps them in the faith, preserves them from straying, and ultimately perfects them (1 Pet. 1:5; Jude 24). We may be confident that God will finish the work of grace He has begun in us (Ps. 138:8; Phil. 1:6; Heb. 12:2). Believers are preserved through Christ's intercession (Luke 22:32; John 17:5) and the ministry of the Holy Spirit (John 14:16; 1 John 2:27).

Perseverance itself, however, is the saints' life-long activity. By faith they confess Christ as Savior (Rom. 10:9), bring forth the fruits of grace (John 15:16), and endure to the end (Matt. 10:22; Heb. 10:28, 29). True believers persevere in the 'things that accompany salvation' (Heb. 6:9) through active faith. God does not deal with them 'as unaccountable automatons, but as moral agents', said A. W. Pink;[23] believers are active in sanctification (Phil. 2:12). They keep themselves from sin (1 John 5:18). They keep themselves in the love of God (Jude 21). They run with patience the race that is set before them (Heb. 12:1). That is how the saints persevere in faith. Christians who say they belong to Christ and yet never lift a finger to purify themselves are deceived. The Christian life inevitably involves putting off the old way of living and putting on the new (Col. 3:8-12).

Saints do this only because of the preserving activity of God the Holy Spirit at work in them (Phil. 2:13). Even so, perseverance includes but extends beyond preservation. Faith in God and His preservation works perseverance in the saints. Moreover, God Himself strengthens the faith of His saints so that they will persevere through all the afflictions appointed to them.[24]

Assurance, Then Perseverance

The fruits of assurance promote perseverance. 'Of the preservation of the elect to salvation and of their perseverance in the faith, true believers for themselves may and do obtain assurance, according to the measure of their faith, whereby they arrive at the certain persuasion that they ever will continue true and living members of the church; and that they experience forgiveness of sins, and will at last inherit eternal life' (*Canons of Dort*, Fifth Head, Art. 9).

The *Canons* affirm that believers 'may and do' obtain assurance of their perseverance. That assurance, however, is grounded in 'the

---

23) A. W. Pink, *The Saint's Perseverance* (MacDill, Fla.: Tyndale Bible Society, n.d.), 11.

24) Goodwin, *Works*, 9:233.

preservation of the elect unto salvation'. Take away those words, and every conscientious believer would despair. Failures in duty would overwhelm whatever fruits we might discover, and destroy all assurance. By speaking first of God's election and preservation, the Canons show that assurance is rooted in God's sovereign grace and promises – yes, in God Himself.

Assurance helps the believer persevere, first, by encouraging him to rest on God's grace in Christ and His promises in the gospel; and second, by presenting these as a powerful motive for Christian living. As Puritan Thomas Goodwin said, assurance 'makes a man work for God ten times more than before'. It 'causes the heart to be more thankful, and more fruitfully and cheerfully obedient; it perfects love, opens and gives vent to a new stream of godly sorrow, adds new motives, enlarges and encourages the heart in prayer, winds up all graces to a new and higher key and strain, causing a spring tide of all'.[25]

Perseverance, Then Assurance

The *Westminster Confession* also presents the close relationship between assurance and perseverance. However, it works from perseverance of the saints (Chap. 17) to assurance of grace and salvation (Chap. 18). This order implies:

First, perseverance opens the way for assurance. If one does not believe in the perseverance of the saints, he cannot be sure he is going to heaven. He may know he is in a state of grace, but he has no way of knowing whether he will continue in that state. Assurance is wedded to the doctrine of perseverance.

Second, perseverance serves to confirm and increase assurance. Those who persist in doing the works that spring from faith will attain high levels of assurance (cf. WCF, 17.2 to 18.2, 17.3 to 18.4).

Third, perseverance causes the believer to live in hope. As believers persevere, they become increasingly confident of victory in Christ and their future with Him in glory (Rom. 5:1-11). As

---

25) Goodwin, *Works*, 1:251.

G. C. Berkouwer said, 'The perseverance of the saints is unbreakably connected with the assurance of faith, in which the believer faces the future with confidence – not with the idea that all dangers and threats have been removed, but rather with the assurance that they shall be conquered indeed.'[26]

Either Way, It Is All by God's Grace

Perseverance and assurance are two sides of one coin. You cannot persevere in grace without growing in assurance, and you cannot grow in assurance of faith without perseverance.

This growth isn't easily attained, but it is attainable through God's grace. 'The Scripture moreover testifies that believers in this life have to struggle with various carnal doubts and that under grievous temptations they are not always sensible of this full assurance of faith and certainty of persevering. But God, who is the Father of all consolation, does not suffer them to be tempted above that they are able, but will with the temptation also make a way to escape that they may be able to bear it (2 Cor. 10:13), and by the Holy Spirit again inspires them with the comfortable assurance of persevering' (*Canons of Dort*, Fifth Head, Art. 11).

With this 'comfortable assurance of persevering', we, with John Newton, can sing of God's 'amazing grace':

> *Through many dangers, toils and snares, I have*
> *already come:*
> *'Tis grace that brought me safe thus far, and grace*
> *will lead me home.*

---

26) G. C. Berkouwer, *Faith and Perseverance* (Grand Rapids: Eerdmans, 1973), 257.

❦ 12 ❦

Conclusion

Tens of thousands of people today say they are assured that Christ is their Savior, yet give little or no evidence that they have been spiritually awakened from the dead. They do not truly *need* Jesus as living Savior and Lord, and remain unresponsive to His spiritual beauty and glory. Unlike Paul, they don't count everything loss for the sake of the excellency and surpassing worth of knowing Christ Jesus as the altogether lovely Bridegroom and Lord (Phil. 3:8). John Piper describes this problem well in a Puritan-like way:

> When these people say they 'receive Christ,' they do not receive him as *supremely valuable*. They receive him simply as sin-forgiver (because they love being guilt-free), and as rescuer-from-hell (because they love being pain-free), and as healer (because they love being disease-free), and as protector (because they love being safe), and as prosperity-giver (because they love being wealthy), and as Creator (because they want a personal universe), and as Lord of history (because they want order and purpose); but they don't receive him as supremely and personally valuable for who he is.

Piper then exhorts solemnly:

> They don't receive him as he really is – more glorious, more beautiful, more wonderful, more satisfying, than everything else in the universe. They don't prize *him*, or treasure *him*, or cherish *him*, or delight in *him*. Or to say it another way, they 'receive Christ' in a way that requires

no change in human nature. You don't have to be born again to love being guilt-free and pain-free and disease-free and safe and wealthy. All natural men without any spiritual life love these things. But to embrace Jesus as your supreme treasure requires a new nature. No one does this naturally. You must be born again (John 3:3). You must be a new creation in Christ (2 Cor. 5:17; Gal. 6:15). You must be made spiritually alive (Eph. 2:1-4).[1]

Anthony Burgess and the Westminster divines fleshed out the doctrine of assurance with precision to undeceive the false professor of faith, to awaken the unsaved, to mature the young in grace, and to comfort the mature in faith. The terminology they developed, their treatises on assurance, their pastoral overtones of compassion for the weak in faith, and their pressing admonitions and invitations to grow in faith showed their great appreciation for vital union and communion with Christ. Scholars today who attribute morbid introspection and man-centeredness to seventeenth-century Puritans have missed the mark. Most Puritan divines examined spiritual experience microscopically because they were eager to trace the faithful track record of God in their lives so they could attribute glory to the Father who elects and provides, the Son who redeems and intercedes, and the Spirit who applies and sanctifies.[2]

Some Puritans spoke of assurance like the breeze that usually blows by the sea, even if at times as only a gentle whisper. Others use the term *assurance* as if it is the mighty wind that propels forward a fully loaded sailing ship. In either case, they affirm that the Spirit blows where He wishes, and we can neither comprehend nor contain Him (John 3:8).

Sometimes the Puritans wrote of assurance in biblically mystical strains of exulting in the love of God through Christ in the Spirit. At other times, they described assurance as the result of careful

---

1) John Piper, *Think: The Life of the Mind and the Love of God* (Wheaton, Ill.: Crossway, 2010), 71.

2) Cf. J. I. Packer, 'The Puritan Idea of Communion with God', in *Press Toward the Mark* (London: n.p., 1962), 7.

self-examination. Most Puritans kept these emphases in careful balance, but each writer found his own unique way of doing so. These variations are bound together by their repeated return to the promises of Scripture as fulfilled in Jesus Christ and to the reliance on the Word and Spirit for all kinds of assurance. Regardless of how they expound assurance, every Puritan invited a Christian to pursue a deeper, fuller, more satisfying, and more sanctified assurance of God's smile upon his life.

If you are not a believer, I pray God that this book will make you realize how critical it is that you become one. How can you face imminent death and eternity not knowing whether you are in Christ or not? You could be in hell tonight. Shake off your sluggishness, cry out to God for mercy, and don't rest until you can say that you belong to the Lord and He belongs to you.

It is important to realize, however, that you don't become a believer by looking for assurance first. You become a believer (1) by realizing your sinfulness and need for Christ, so that you cry out for mercy (Luke 18:13); (2) by recognizing that the way to Christ is wide open and accessible, since He is an approachable Savior who loves to receive and save sinners (Luke 15:2); and (3) by casting yourself upon Him with all your sins, believing and trusting in Him alone for salvation (Acts 16:31, 34). Read the beautiful lyrics of Joseph Hart's hymn 'Come and Welcome to Jesus Christ' carefully and prayerfully, and then come to Jesus just as you are by His own inviting and alluring grace:

> *Come ye sinners, poor and wretched,*
> *Weak and wounded, sick and sore,*
> *Jesus ready stands to save you,*
> *Full of pity, joined with power.*
> *He is able, He is willing,*
> *Doubt no more.*
>
> *Let not conscience make you linger,*
> *Nor of fitness fondly dream*
> *All the fitness He requires*

Is to feel your need of Him.
This He gives you,
'Tis the Spirit's rising beam

Come ye weary, heavy laden,
Lost and ruined by the fall;
If you wait until you're better
You will never come at all.
Not the righteous but sinners,
Jesus came to call.[3]

Is it the longing of your heart to come to Jesus in this way? The way is wide open. There are no obstacles. All the fitness He requires is 'to feel your need of Him'. I would urge you not to delay. Place your eternal welfare in His care. He holds out His arms to receive you. Do you believe that? That is the gospel: 'Jesus ready stands to save you.' How many times has He pleaded with you to come, but you spurned His invitation? How many times have you turned your back on a pleading Savior because you did not feel fit to come to Him? You wanted to bring something to Him, but you cannot come that way. Don't ever do this again. Come to a pleading, inviting Savior just as you are, casting yourself upon Him, resting in Him alone for full and free salvation. He will not turn you away. When you do this, you will soon know by experience that faith is a gift of God.

Yes, you may reply, but what if God has decreed me only to be a seeker and not a finder? I know that I need the Lord. I have no doubt about the doctrine of justification by faith alone. I know the remedy and I believe in its efficacy. But I still wrestle with the personal application of salvation: Can I truly be saved? May I, too, wash and be clean? What if I am not elected?

My friend, divine election is not the enemy but the friend of sinners. Without divine election, there would be no hope for anyone, for we are all sinners. Because of election, sinners and seekers are

---

3) Joseph Hart, 'Come and Welcome to Jesus Christ', https://www.opc.org/hymn.html?hymn_id=143

always welcome with God. There is not a single verse in all the Bible that tells you that you will not be welcomed by God when you cast yourself with all your sins at His feet and put all your trust in His Son. The last invitation of the Bible says, 'Whosoever will, let him take the water of life freely' (Rev. 22:17). After quoting that text, Charles Spurgeon wrote,

> Does that exclude you? It is written, Whosoever shall call upon the name of the Lord shall be saved. Does that shut you out? No, it includes you; it invites you; it encourages you. Nowhere in the Word of God is it written that you will be cast out if you come. Or that Jesus Christ will not remove your burden of sin if you come and lay it at His feet. A thousand passages of Scripture welcome you. Not one stands with a drawn sword to keep you back from the Tree of Life. Our heavenly Father sets His angels at the gates of His house to welcome all comers.[4]

Don't let election rob you of comfort but let it give you hope. Listen to Spurgeon who answered this objection so helpfully in one of his sermons:

> Seeker, if you find yourself in the garden of the household of God you have not come here as an intruder, for the gate is open and it is God's will that you should come. If you receive Christ into your heart you will not have stolen treasure. It was God's will that you should receive Christ. If, with broken heart, you come and rest on the finished sacrifice of Jesus, you need not fear that you will violate the eternal purpose of God, or come into collision with the divine decree of God. It is God's will that brought you into that condition. This is why conviction of sin is so important for us. God brought you into that condition of realization that you are a sinner. You didn't do this yourself. It was the work of the Holy Spirit of God. It was all part of God's foreordained eternal counsel in your life before time. One of the most groundless fears a person can entertain is the dread that the Father will be unwilling to forgive. If you desire, God has long ago desired it to be so. If you determine in your heart to find God, He has long ago determined it for

---

4) Charles Spurgeon, *Advice for Seekers* (Edinburgh: Banner of Truth Trust, 2016), 25–6.

you. You need never be troubled about predestination. If you come to Christ and cast yourself upon Him, you need not entertain a fear that you are violating the will of God because salvation is the will of God which Jesus Christ has come to fulfill.[5]

If you are a believer, I pray that the *Westminster Confession*'s statements on assurance, particularly as fleshed out by Anthony Burgess, will assist you in making your calling and election sure by going beyond yourself to find everything necessary for your salvation in this life and the better eternal life to come in the Spirit-applied grace of God in Jesus Christ. For Burgess, that is a worthy goal. Assurance is an excellent privilege because it provides numerous graces so beneficial for a close walk with God, such as an evangelical frame of heart, submission and assistance in the midst of trials and troubles, enlargement of prayer, a tenderness of conscience against sin, a daily resting in God's dear Son, and a patient yet impatient longing for Christ's second coming.[6] Perhaps Burroughs said it best when he wrote that our duty is to labor for the assurance of God's love, for 'it will assist us in all duties; it will arm us against all temptations; it will answer all objections that can be made against the soul's peace; it will sustain us in all conditions, into which the saddest of times may bring us'.[7]

To know full assurance of faith is one of life's greatest joys. 'Assurance is glory in the bud, it is the suburbs of paradise, it is a cluster of the land of promise, it is a spark of God, it is the joy and crown of a Christian', wrote Brooks.[8] The great nineteenth-century hymnist Fanny Crosby was physically blind, but spiritually she was embraced and was engulfed by life's most steadfast love – the love of the triune God in Jesus Christ, which she poeticized in her classic hymn, 'Blessed Assurance':

---

5) Charles Spurgeon, *Sunlight for Cloudy Days* (London: Wakeman Trust, 2014), 8–9.

6) *Spiritual Refining*, 26.

7) Burroughs, *An Exposition of the Prophecy of Hosea*, 654. Cf. Gillespie, *A Treatise of Miscellany Questions*, 57.

8) Brooks, *Heaven on Earth*, 30.

Blessed assurance, Jesus is mine!
Oh, what a foretaste of glory divine!
Heir of salvation, purchase of God,
Born of His Spirit, washed in His blood.

Perfect submission, all is at rest,
I in my Savior am happy and blest,
Watching and waiting, looking above,
Filled with His goodness, lost in His love.

This is my story, this is my song,
Praising my Savior all the day long;
This is my story, this is my song,
Praising my Savior all the day long.[9]

What about you? Is this joy of blessed assurance real for you? Despite your struggles, is this also the goal of your life? Are you personally acquainted with saving faith, and are you praying for increasing measures of blessed assurance in Christ, even if, as Calvin said, 'unbelief will not down'?[10]

Be thankful for the assurance that you do have. Question your Father's love no more. Rejoice as an adopted child of God; refuse to regress back to slavish fears. Keep your garments pure.[11] Let your measure of assurance be reflected in your daily life.

Let us live out each day the lessons Burgess and the Puritans teach us: Our primary ground of assurance is in the promises of God in Christ. Those promises must be applied to our hearts, must bear fruit in our lives, and help us experience the Spirit's corroborating witness with our spirit that we are indeed sons of God. Daily we are called to live fruitful lives, to speak well of our great assuring God, and to serve as salt in the earth.

---

9) Fanny Crosby, 'Blessed Assurance', https://www.google.com/search?q=Lyrics+of+Blessed+Assurance

10) Calvin, *Institutes of the Christian Religion*, 3.2.15.

11) Cf. Brooks, *Heaven on Earth*, 317–20.

The practical message for the true Christian is simply this: Faith ultimately must triumph because it comes from the triune God and rests on His Word; let us therefore not despair when, for a time, we do not feel its triumph. Let us more fully embrace God's promise in Christ, recognizing that our certainty, both objective and subjective, lies wholly in Christ, for faith is of Christ and rests in Him.

Christ shall ultimately win the day in believers, for it is He, Calvin wrote, who 'wishes to cure the disease [of unbelief] in us, so that among us He may obtain full faith in His promises'.[12] Let us take courage and seek grace to honor Christ, and through Christ, God Triune, for ultimately, our assurance is not about self-confidence but about confidence in the Father, the Son, and the Spirit. That is what Scripture, faith and assurance, Calvin and Reformed theology, Burgess and Puritanism, yes, and life itself are all about – honoring the triune God through Jesus Christ. 'For of him, and through him, and to him, are all things: to whom be glory for ever. Amen' (Rom. 11:36).

---

12) Calvin, *Institutes of the Christian Religion*, 3.2.15.

Appendix 1

WESTMINSTER CONFESSION OF FAITH
Chapter 18

1. Although hypocrites and other unregenerate men may vainly deceive themselves with false hopes, and carnal presumptions of being in the favour of God, and estate of salvation; which hope of theirs shall perish: yet such as truly believe in the Lord Jesus, and love Him in sincerity, endeavouring to walk in all good conscience before Him, may, in this life, be certainly assured that they are in the state of grace, and may rejoice in the hope of the glory of God, which hope shall never make them ashamed.

2. This certainty is not a bare conjectural and probable persuasion, grounded upon a fallible hope; but an infallible assurance of faith, founded upon the divine truth of the promises of salvation, the inward evidence of those graces unto which these promises are made, the testimony of the Spirit of adoption witnessing with our spirits that we are the children of God: which Spirit is the earnest of our inheritance, whereby we are sealed to the day of redemption.

3. This infallible assurance doth not so belong to the essence of faith, but that a true believer may wait long, and conflict with many difficulties before he be partaker of it: yet, being enabled by the Spirit to know the things which are freely given him of God, he may without extraordinary revelation, in the right use of ordinary means, attain thereunto. And therefore it is the duty of everyone to give all diligence to make his calling and election sure; that thereby his heart may be enlarged in peace and joy in the Holy Ghost, in

love and thankfulness to God, and in strength and cheerfulness in the duties of obedience, the proper fruits of this assurance: so far is it from inclining men to looseness.

4. True believers may have the assurance of their salvation divers ways shaken, diminished, and intermitted; as, by negligence in preserving of it, by falling into some special sin, which woundeth the conscience and grieveth the Spirit; by some sudden or vehement temptation, by God's withdrawing the light of His countenance, suffering even such as fear Him to walk in darkness and to have no light; yet are they never utterly destitute of that seed of God, and life of faith, that love of Christ and the brethren, that sincerity of heart, and conscience of duty, out of which, by the operation of the Spirit, this assurance may, in due time, be revived; and by the which, in the mean time, they are supported from utter despair.

Appendix 2

Three Kinds of Assurance	Holy Scripture	Canons of Dort (1619)	Westminster Confession (1647)
Primary Ground: The Promises of the Gospel	'For all the promises of God in Him are Yea, and in Him Amen, unto the glory of God by us' (2 Cor. 1:20).	'Assurance... springs from faith in God's promises, which He has most abundantly revealed in His Word for our comfort...' (V, 10).	'...the divine truth of the promises of salvation' (18.2).
Secondary Ground #1: Inward evidences of Fruits of Saving Grace	'And hereby we do know that we know Him, if we keep His commandments' (1 John 2:3).	'Assurance... springs...from a serious and holy desire to preserve a good conscience and to perform good works...' (V, 10; cf. 1, 12; V, error 5).	'...the inward evidence of those graces unto which these promises are made...' (18.2).
Secondary Ground #2 The Testimony of the Holy Spirit	'Ye have received the Spirit of adoption, whereby we cry, Abba, Father. The Spirit itself beareth witness with our spirit, that we are the children of God' (Rom. 8:15b-16).	'assurance... springs...from the testimony of the Holy Spirit witnessing with our Spirit that we are children and heirs of God...' (V, 10).	'...the testimony of the Spirit of adoption witnessing with our spirits that we are the children of God...' (18.2).

ASSURANCE
How to know you are a Christian

J.C. RYLE

Assurance
by J. C. Ryle

It is right to have confidence in your Christian life, if that confidence stems from God's saving power. J. C. Ryle shows us that assurance is something every Christian should desire. There are steps we can take in our search for that goal; these are clearly marked out for us by Ryle. Do you know that you are part of God's family?

ISBN: 978-1-87167-605-1

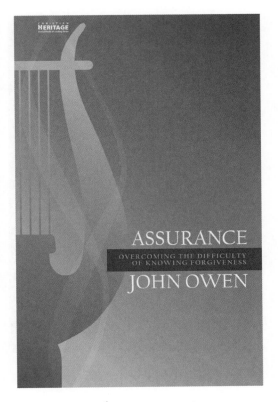

Assurance
Overcoming the Difficulty of Knowing Forgiveness
by John Owen

How can I be sure that God has forgiven me? In this volume, essentially an exposition of Psalm 130, John Owen pinpoints the causes of such spiritual distress, not merely with the clinical skill of a spiritual diagnostician, but also with the understanding of someone who had profound experience of those 'depths'. And Owen does not stop with diagnosis. He maps out a biblical path of faith and obedience for distressed believers who long to say with full assurance, 'God has forgiven me.'

ISBN: 978-1-84550-974-3

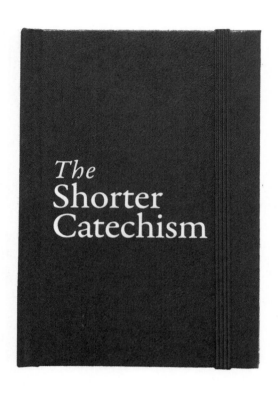

The Shorter Catechism
by Roderick Lawson

The Westminster Assembly of 1643 to 1649 produced three documents of lasting value to the Church: The Westminster Confession of Faith, The Larger Catechism, and The Shorter Catechism. Since then, The Shorter Catechism has become well known as a manual of doctrine for both children and adults who require an introduction to the Christian faith. It is an ideal way to give structure to the discipling of new believers. This edition contains the addition of Scripture proof texts and notes by Roderick Lawson.

ISBN: 978-1-78191-810-4

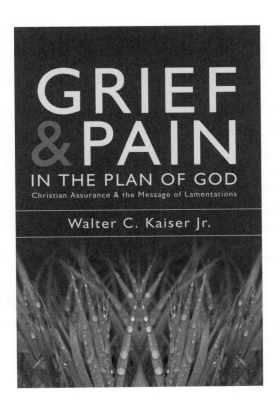

Grief and Pain in the Plan of God
Christian Assurance and the message of Lamentations
by Walter C. Kaiser Jr.

How are we to understand suffering and its place in our lives? Should we try and rationalise it away, trying to come up with a solution that sits as comfortably as possible? Surely we should look to Scripture first? This is what Walter Kaiser does here. Looking at the Old Testament book of Lamentations Kaiser does not offer any easy solutions – but rather shows us how a Sovereign and Loving God can work through even the most painful moments.

ISBN: 978-1-85792-993-5

Christian Focus Publications

Our mission statement –

STAYING FAITHFUL

In dependence upon God we seek to impact the world through literature faithful to His infallible Word, the Bible. Our aim is to ensure that the Lord Jesus Christ is presented as the only hope to obtain forgiveness of sin, live a useful life and look forward to heaven with Him.

Our books are published in four imprints:

CHRISTIAN
FOCUS

Popular works including biographies, commentaries, basic doctrine and Christian living.

CHRISTIAN
HERITAGE

Books representing some of the best material from the rich heritage of the church.

MENTOR

Books written at a level suitable for Bible College and seminary students, pastors, and other serious readers. The imprint includes commentaries, doctrinal studies, examination of current issues and church history.

CF4•K

Children's books for quality Bible teaching and for all age groups: Sunday school curriculum, puzzle and activity books; personal and family devotional titles, biographies and inspirational stories – because you are never too young to know Jesus!

Christian Focus Publications Ltd,
Geanies House, Fearn, Ross-shire,
IV20 1TW, Scotland, United Kingdom.
www.christianfocus.com
blog.christianfocus.com